THE CENTENARY BOOK OF SARK

A history and description of the artist William A Toplis R A and making both the 1908 and Centenary Editions of the book.

A new edition of the 1908 classic. Republished and printed using the original 100 year old copper halftone plates for the 21 colour illustrations and letterpress printing for the text. Printed on archival quality material throughout. Full vellum or cloth bound and presented in a full cloth solander box with this accompanying volume.

PUBLISHED BY
GATEWAY PUBLISHING LTD, SARK

The Book of Sark Centenary Edition and this commentary volume
are published by

Gateway Publishing Ltd
PO Box 31
Sark
Channel Islands
GY9 0SB
www.bookofsark.com
Tel +44(0)1865 723404

Title page picture: Port Gouray

ACKNOWLEDGEMENTS

The Commentary Volume

Text by Chris Andrews, Fiona Kelly and Amy McKee, with thanks for
material supplied by Paul Toplis
Photography by Chris Andrews, with additions from Richard Axton,
William Raymond and Reese Andrews
Design by Mike Brain Graphic Design Limited
Edited by Amy McKee
Printed by J F Print Ltd, Sparkford

The Book of Sark Centenary Edition

Plates printed by The Logan Press, Wellingborough
Text set by Gloucester Typsetting, printed by Evergreen Press, both of Stroud
Mould made paper from St Cuthbert's Mill, Somerset
Vellum and cloth binding by Derry's of Nottingham
Solander box and book block by The Fine Book Bindery, Wellingborough
The Book reproduces the original contributions of William Arthur Toplis,
John Oxenham, T G Bonney and E D Marquand

The production of *The Book of Sark Centenary Edition* and this Commentary Volume owe a great deal to the help of people on Sark and Guernsey, including the Société Serquaise and Guernsey Museum & Galleries. Particular thanks to the Kelly family including the William A Toplis great-granddaughter Fiona for carefully preserving the 100 year old printing plates and for their constant enthusiasm and help with the project. To Sark Island, Guernsey Museum & Galleries and the Private Collection at Mount Stuart, Isle of Bute for permission to reproduce photographs of the Toplis paintings in their collection. Finally many thanks for the support and attention to detail of Duncan Spence

Contents

Section 1
William Arthur Toplis

The Artist, The Man (1857–1942)

William Arthur Toplis was a successful twenty-six year old artist whose work had already been accepted for exhibition by the Royal Academy in London when he first arrived in Sark in 1883, on what was supposed to be a two-week family holiday. This holiday – a gift from some of his more affluent and generous friends – was to last almost sixty years and formed the basis for most of his life's work.

Toplis and his wife, Nellie, were living in Jersey with their two very young children and Arthur, as he was known to his family, was painting with hopes of gaining further acceptance into the Royal Academy Exhibitions in London. He had already had two paintings accepted by the Academy, 'Sermons in Stone', in 1880 and 'Granite Rocks, Jersey', in 1881.

When he arrived in Sark, Toplis spent many hours rambling around the Island with his three friends, Feeney, Johnstone, and Hayes, enjoying the unusual topography and lush scenery. The steep cliffs around the perimeter of the Island are often dotted with hundreds of varieties of wild flowers that grow on the Island. On the sixth day of his holiday in Sark, Toplis encountered the magnificent Coupée between Big Sark and Little Sark. At the time Toplis first saw it the Coupée was a narrow natural isthmus topped by a crude and crumbling track as wide as a horse-drawn cart, and stretching a hundred yards to join Big Sark with Little Sark. Although it has now been paved and turned into a safer roadway, it is probably still the Island's most outstanding natural feature. On the Jersey side, the Coupée plunges three hundred feet almost straight down into the dark and sinister-looking Coupée Bay. On the other side, facing Guernsey, luxuriant foliage covers the steep but accessible cliff-side leading down to the sandy beach of Grande Grève. Toplis decided immediately upon seeing it that he would not leave Sark until he had captured the view from the Guernsey side on canvas. Without consulting his wife, he sent to Jersey for their possessions and rented a house on Sark.

The Coupée in the late 19th century as Toplis would have seen it

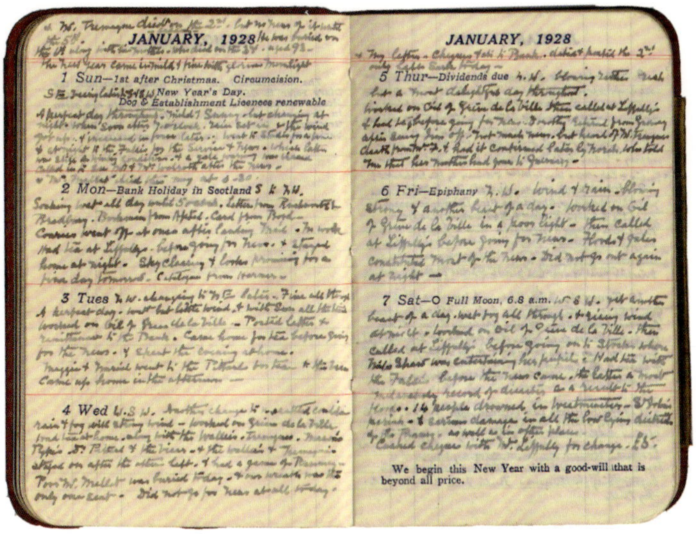

Toplis, when in his 80s and pages from his meticulously kept diaries

A complex man who was meticulous about his stamps, his paintings, and his record-keeping, Toplis did not settle easily among the farmers and fishermen of Sark and almost immediately became a controversial figure who never hesitated to embrace any cause that struck him as morally unjust. He spent much time and money advancing or defending various causes, many of which were personal, although he was untrained in the law and had only a layman's knowledge of certain aspects of English law. He failed to grasp the fact that Sark was not governed by the same civil laws as England, a failing which was to cause him and his family much distress and hardship over the years as he managed to alienate many of the Island's inhabitants including most of its leaders. This alienation led to a steady stream of arrests and legal actions, as well as personal attacks against Toplis and his family members. Despite this rather uneasy relationship with many of the Islanders, Toplis and several of his family spent the rest of their lives in Sark.

Although physically of small stature – a thin and wiry five feet three inches tall – Toplis had a reputation for being energetic, determined, and persistent, with an ability to disregard personal hardship in order to satisfy his own aims. He is variously described as being charming, considerate, a devoted father and grandfather, and conversely being selfish, self-centered, secretive, quarrelsome, and bad-tempered. There is evidence that he showed little consideration for his wife when, without consulting her about moving to Sark, he consigned her to what she often referred to as 'my Sark exile.' He showed a relentless drive for perfection and an obsession with detail and accuracy in every aspect of his life. He kept copious notes and diaries recording even the most minute details about the seasons, the times, the tides and all aspects of the weather when he was painting.

Mr and Mrs William Arthur Toplis

Early Life

EVENING PRESS, SATURDAY, OCTOBER 22, 1938

HE KNEW CHARLES DICKENS

Mr. and Mrs. Toplis Celebrate Diamond Wedding

A GREAT ARTIST LOOKS BACK

Visited Sark 55 Years Ago for Holiday

HAS REMAINED THERE EVER SINCE

Newspaper cutting (courtesy of *The Guernsey Press*)

Toplis was born on 24th March, 1857, in Sheffield, England. He was one of six children and the second youngest of William and Eliza Toplis. He had an elder brother who was eighteen years his senior, but this brother was disowned by the family and Thomas, seventeen years older than Arthur, was regarded as the eldest.

Toplis' father was a manufacturer and supplier of picture frames and his mother was the daughter of a professor of music, 'professor' being a title not necessarily indicating academic status within a university but commonly bestowed on those who were involved in a 'cultural profession'. As a young boy, he was greatly influenced by the tastes and interests of his mother and grandmother, often spending evenings at literary readings and concerts, thus developing an intense love of music and literature. Toplis frequently listened to readings of Charles Dickens' work, and he liked to tell that he sat on Dickens' knee listening to Dickens' accounts of his travels and was particularly intrigued by stories about the Channel Islands. Dickens became a schoolboy hero to the young Toplis and it was perhaps these stories that started his interest in the Islands.

SCIENCE AND ART DEPARTMENT OF THE COMMITTEE OF COUNCIL ON EDUCATION.

CERTIFICATE OF THE SECOND GRADE.

I Hereby Certify that

Wm Arthur Toplis

has passed a satisfactory examination in—

Freehand Drawing.
Practical Geometry.
Linear Perspective.
Model Drawing.

Official Inspector.

Certificate granted 18th day of June 1872

By order of the Committee of Council on Education.

No 2642

Toplis' leaving certificate from Sheffield School of Art, 1872

As a child, Toplis attended Bowlings School followed by the People's College in Sheffield. He was given a box of paints, palette, and easel by his grandmother for Christmas 1867. Until that time, his primary hobby had been stamp collecting, but this interest soon took second place to sketching and painting. He sold his first painting at the age of ten and soon thereafter entered the Sheffield School of Art from which he earned a graduation certificate at the age of fifteen. He studied black and white drawing under W H Sounes but was never formally taught the use of colour. However, he had a good eye for colour and an innate talent for matching colours exactly which enabled him to mix colours to perfectly match his subjects. His personal preference was for strong, intense colours which he used to good effect in his landscapes.

Stamp Collecting

Toplis developed an interest in stamp collecting whilst a child at home, continuing throughout his life and in this he was as detailed in his approach and recording as he was in his painting. Upon his death

Toplis left an impressive collection, sadly broken up and partly lost, but it was estimated that if still intact, it would have had a current catalogue value in excess of four million pounds.

Paintings

Almost the entire body of Toplis' work consists of landscapes with particular attention paid to rocks, which is perhaps why the landscape of Sark held such appeal for him. Throughout his work, living creatures were rarely included in his paintings. Early in his career when he included a drawing of a horse in a landscape, a lady wrote to tell him that his representation bore no resemblance whatsoever to any living creature – and from that time onwards, he made almost no attempt to include animals or people in his work. The occasional seagull appears in some seascapes but these still appear slightly incongruous and mechanical. The inclusion of limpets seems less unusual as they tend to remain in situ for considerable time, almost as if part of the rocks themselves.

Additionally, it is interesting to note that very few of his paintings include any man-made structure or object, the notable exceptions being Creux Harbour, Old Well at Dixcart and Baleine Bay, the latter with the inclusion of a small '*dilapidated shed*' near his studio when he lived in the Barracks in Little Sark. Also, the one picture of movement – A Sark Souffleur (Saignée Bay) – is as unusual as is the inclusion of the female figure in Venus Bath. Venus Bath is the only known Toplis painting to include a human form and this one human figure took him many years to complete.

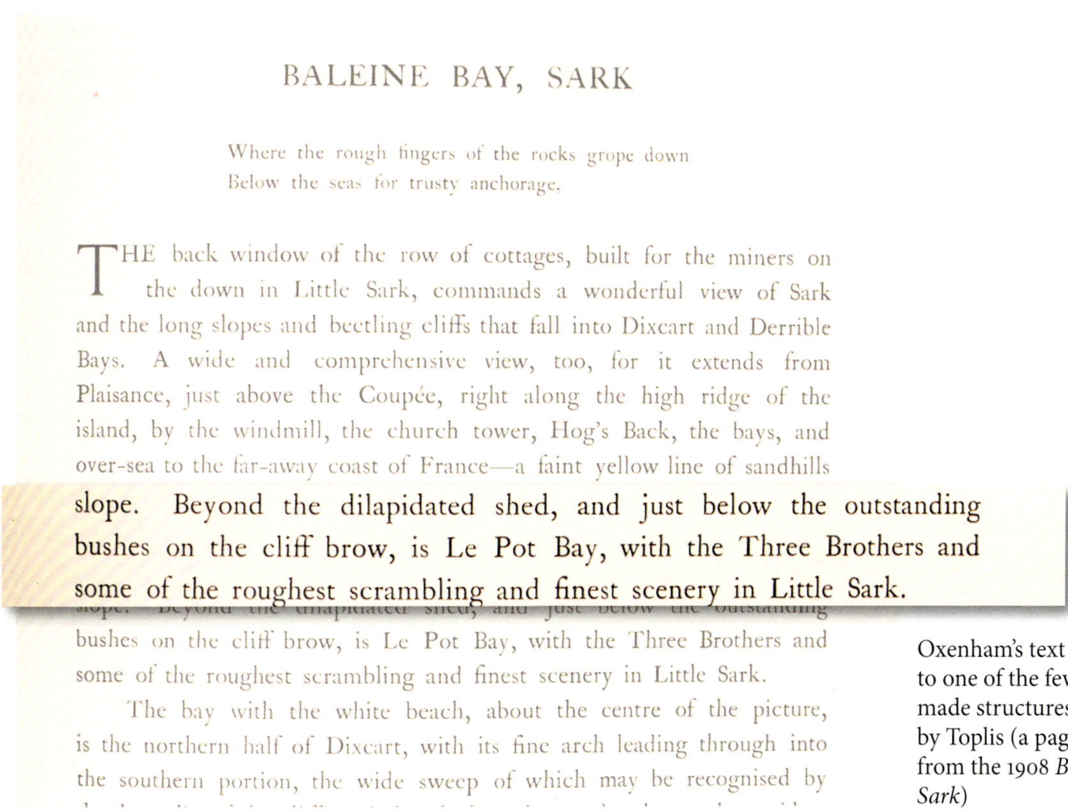

BALEINE BAY, SARK

Where the rough fingers of the rocks grope down
Below the seas for trusty anchorage.

THE back window of the row of cottages, built for the miners on the down in Little Sark, commands a wonderful view of Sark and the long slopes and beetling cliffs that fall into Dixcart and Derrible Bays. A wide and comprehensive view, too, for it extends from Plaisance, just above the Coupée, right along the high ridge of the island, by the windmill, the church tower, Hog's Back, the bays, and over-sea to the far-away coast of France—a faint yellow line of sandhills

slope. Beyond the dilapidated shed, and just below the outstanding bushes on the cliff brow, is Le Pot Bay, with the Three Brothers and some of the roughest scrambling and finest scenery in Little Sark.

slope. Beyond the dilapidated shed, and just below the outstanding bushes on the cliff brow, is Le Pot Bay, with the Three Brothers and some of the roughest scrambling and finest scenery in Little Sark.

The bay with the white beach, about the centre of the picture, is the northern half of Dixcart, with its fine arch leading through into the southern portion, the wide sweep of which may be recognised by

Oxenham's text referring to one of the few man made structures painted by Toplis (a page copied from the 1908 *Book of Sark*)

Toplis and his Method of Working

To say that Toplis was painstaking in his work would perhaps be an understatement. His attention to detail was so extreme as to almost be obsessive, and he often repainted the same subject many times in an effort to produce an exact representation. One of his contemporaries once commented that if there was a limpet in the pool, Toplis would have included it in his painting.

Toplis kept meticulous records of the tides, the sunrises and sunsets, and weather conditions for many years. This data was recorded in small notebooks, some of which may be seen later in this book.

There is record that many of his paintings took several years to complete. Margaret Waller in her book, *An Artist Recalls Happy Days in Sark*, says, *'Mr. Toplis ... might be described as an artist of the Pre-Raphaelite School. Such was the infinite care and detail he used in his oil paintings.'* She goes on to describe seeing pebbles spread on the floor of his studio which he was using as models from which to paint a perfectly accurate beach foreground.

Many hours have been spent researching the notebooks and visiting the sites of Toplis' paintings, in order to replicate his views by photography as closely as possible. The photographs do show changes

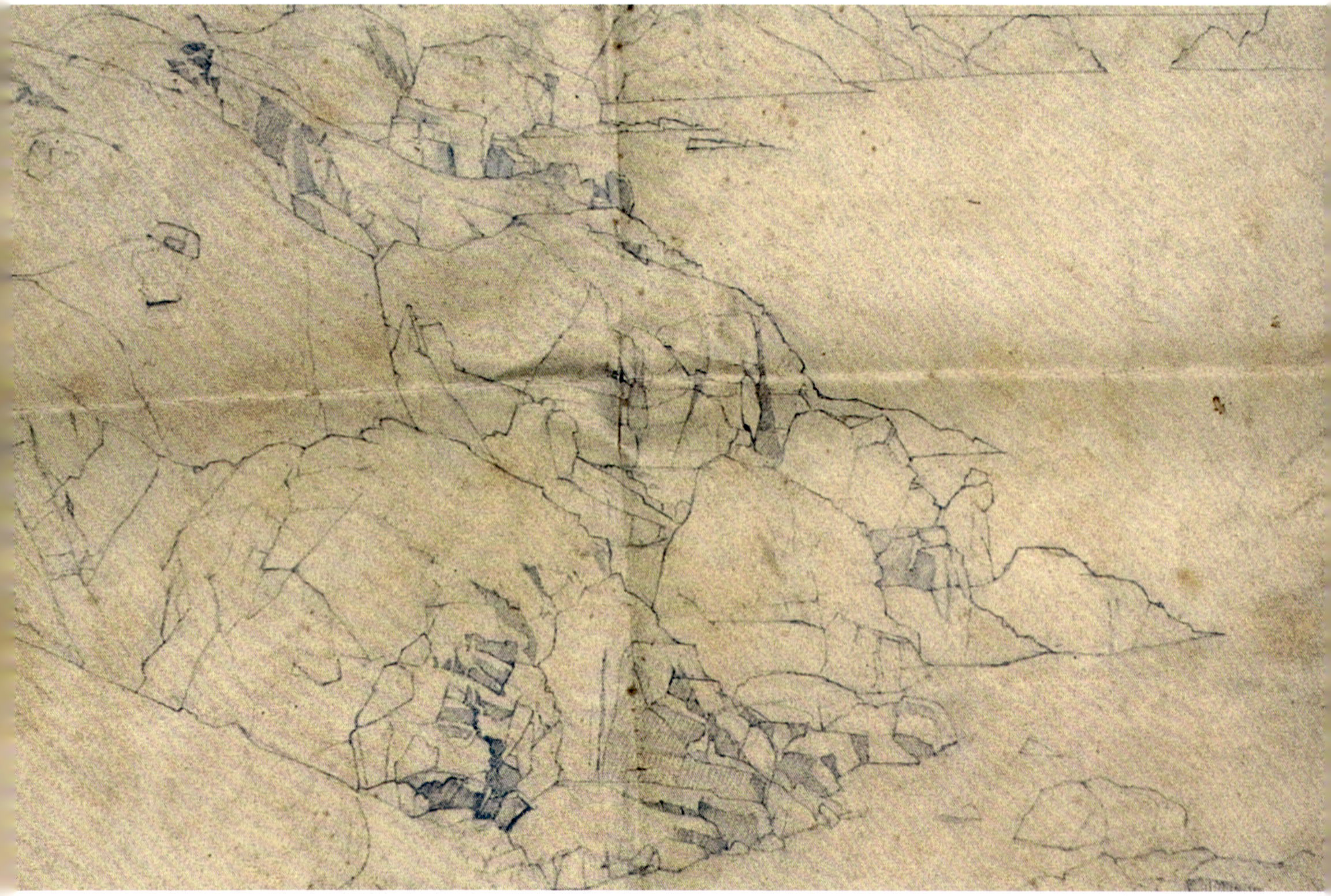

Fine detailed working sketch for 'The West Coast of Sark'

in topography caused by rock falls and landslides, man-made excavations, and general erosion, but it seems highly possible that there is an additional factor to be considered. Margaret Waller says:

'Mr. Toplis' method of painting was to decide upon a certain lighting effect at a certain time of the day, on a certain day of the year. Of course, he could not finish the picture in one day. He would spend two or three days painting a particular subject then, as the sun 'moved around', the shadows would change. Mr. Toplis put his unfinished picture away until the same time the following year! This explains why it could take T.P. twenty years to complete one picture.'

If indeed this is an accurate description of his methodology, the paintings could be a composite of several years' views of each subject, and therefore difficult to replicate with a single photograph. (Margaret Waller seems to use her own shorthand for Toplis as 'T.P.')

The note at the base of the working drawing on the previous page, reading: *'auf weidersehen'* in Toplis' hand. Said to have been done during the war, when he had otherwise almost completely stopped working, Toplis died in 1942

Venus Bath

The painting popularly called Venus Bath has a colourful history and is probably the most unusual painting in *The Book of Sark*. Toplis painted several versions of the subject both before and after the one that appears in *The Book of Sark*.

There are a number of different versions of the story of Toplis' introduction to what has become known as 'Venus Bath' in Little Sark. Some of the Sark guide books credit Toplis with the discovery of the pool but Toplis himself gave that credit to his friend Peregrine M. Feeney. Feeney is also credited with putting forth the idea that Toplis should paint the now-famous pool.

According to Toplis' own records, Feeney took Toplis to the pool one clear morning as the sun was rising. Toplis was captivated by the beauty of the pool and the surrounding rocks. When his friends, Hume and Malan, wrote a guidebook of Sark including the little pool, Toplis told them he had called it 'Feeney's Bath' but they misunderstood him and wrote 'Venus Bath'. The name caught on and Toplis made no effort to correct the error. However it should be noted that in *The Book of Sark* he did not use either name, but labelled the picture as follows:

'Formed and adorned by Nature's wondrous Art, A Sea-shore pool – to 'Venus' dedicate.'

This natural rock pool was visible only from a rock-shelf below a cliff and it was covered by seawater from half-tide onwards. The pool was supposedly unknown to anyone until Feeney discovered it, but how Feeney came to learn of its existence remains a mystery. (It seems unlikely that none of the native

Sarkees knew of it considering the Island's diminutive size). Feeney, a flamboyant character who was himself an artist, felt that he lacked the 'temperament' necessary to undertake a painting of the pool and challenged Toplis to take on this project.

Toplis started his work on Venus Bath in the spring of 1887, but many difficulties impeded his progress on the painting and he spent the next twenty-three years working on it. One of the most frustrating aspects of the work for Toplis was the fact that it was only possible to paint when the receding tide had left the pool surrounded by dry rock and when there were no unfavourable weather conditions. The correct tides and weather conditions also had to coincide with the early morning light to give the desired colouring to the rock and water in the pool. When all conditions were right, the artist would climb down a steep path to the pool with his easel and paints and work for as long as possible, usually only an hour or two. This was contrary to his preferred method of painting which was to paint virtually nonstop for eight hours or more.

Feeney had requested that Toplis include a bathing figure in the painting, and although the oil painting was mostly finished by 1902, there was no human figure. Toplis was apparently becoming increasingly frustrated by this and in desperation in 1904, while in London for the Royal Academy Exhibition, he hired a rather obese, long-haired model to pose for his Venus. His records indicate that she was paid sixpence to pose for him.

After returning to Sark, Toplis painted this figure into his composition but this required changing the rock to create a ledge upon which the figure could sit. Because Toplis never relied on his imagination but rather was known for his accuracy of detail, he was not satisfied with the work. Even so, he submitted it to the Royal Academy in 1907 and in 1908 only to have it rejected both times. Despite these rejections, there was a great deal of interest in the painting and he sent it to Dickinson Studios where black and white prints were made for sale. When he received the prints, he painted over them, giving the figure more hair in an effort to cover what he considered to be the 'unsatisfactory body' of his Venus. He was later to remove this figure completely and add a much smaller, more slender Venus to the composition. It has been suggested that this later model was in fact Oxenham's daughter.

While waiting for inspiration for the figure in the painting, he began a water colour from a slightly different angle. This painting was promised to Emil Sang as partial payment for some postage stamps but due to financial difficulties, Toplis sold the picture to Walter Henty for one hundred guineas, and sent Sang forty guineas and promised to make a smaller copy for him. Needless to say, Sang was not happy as he had already waited four years for the painting.

Finally, Toplis completed a copy of the picture in 1907, but Sang himself was experiencing financial difficulties and he agreed that Toplis should sell the painting to F. Dixon for sixty pounds and send him fifty pounds. Sang then informed Toplis that, *'having waited six years for the picture and been deprived of it twice, he never wanted to see Venus again.'*

This was not the end of the Venus-saga for Sang. A few years later, Toplis painted another watercolour version of this subject which he sent to Sang which, according to Sang's letter of appreciation to Toplis, was received with 'delight'.

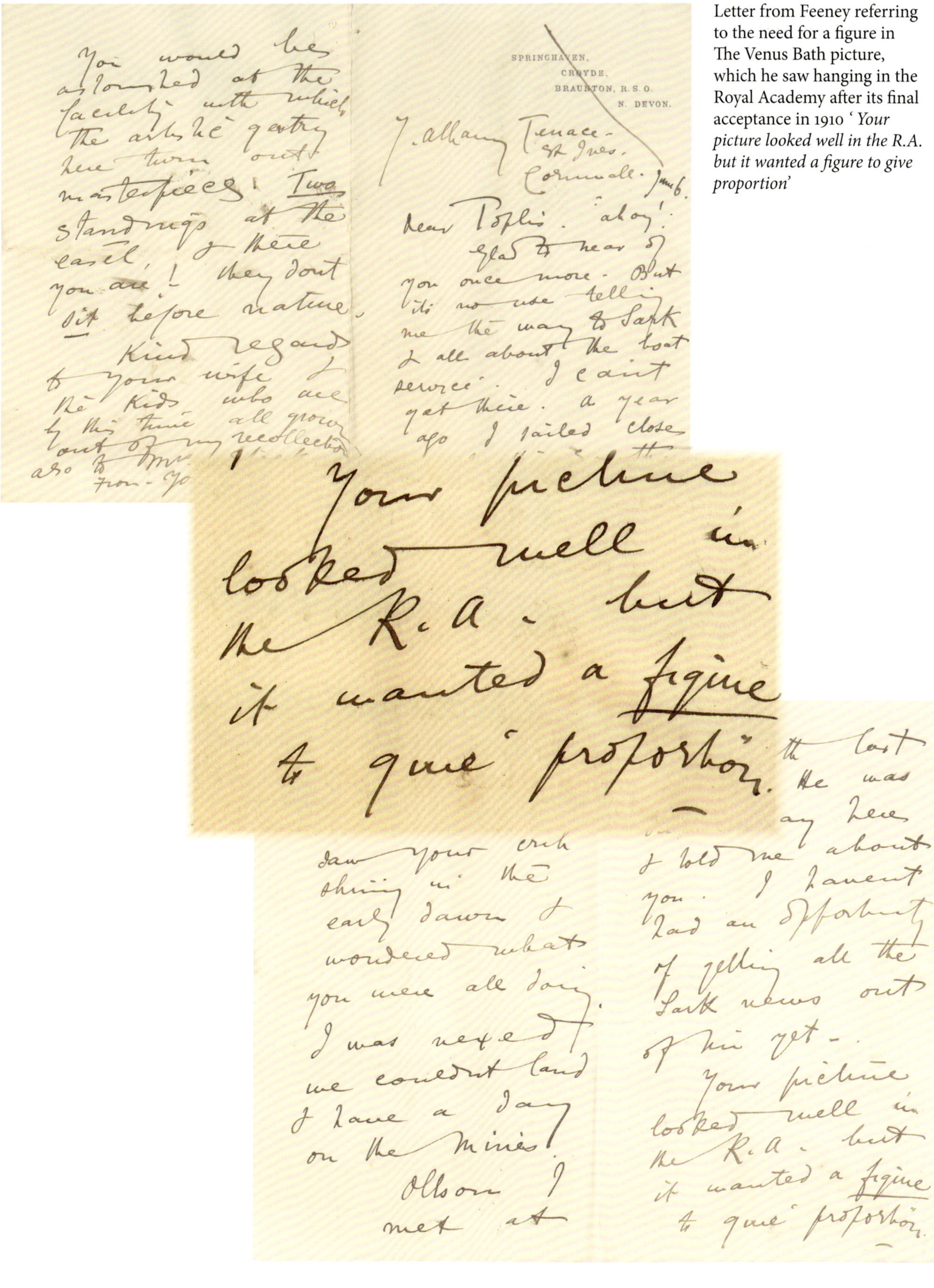

SPRINGHAVEN,
CROYDE,
BRAUNTON, R.S.O.
N. DEVON.

7. Albany Terrace –
St Ives.
Cornwall. June 6.

Dear Toplis. "ahoy"! Glad to hear of you once more. But its no use telling me the way to Sark & all about the boat service. I cant get there. A year ago I sailed close … saw your cush shining in the early dawn & wondered what you were all doing. I was vexed we couldnt land & have a day on the mines! Olsson I met at … the last … He was … here & told me about you. I havent had an opportunity of getting all the Sark news out of him yet. Your picture looked well in the R.A. but it wanted a figure to give proportion.

You would be astonished at the facility with which the artistic gentry here turn out masterpieces! Two sittings at the easel, & there you are! they dont sit before nature.

Kind regards to your wife & the kids who are by this time all grown out of my recollection … from – Yo…

Letter from Feeney referring to the need for a figure in The Venus Bath picture, which he saw hanging in the Royal Academy after its final acceptance in 1910 '*Your picture looked well in the R.A. but it wanted a figure to give proportion*'

Two different photographic prints of the Venus Bath picture, with the original model above, and below, the final version

The original sketch of 'Venus', a great rarity for Toplis to be painting a figure

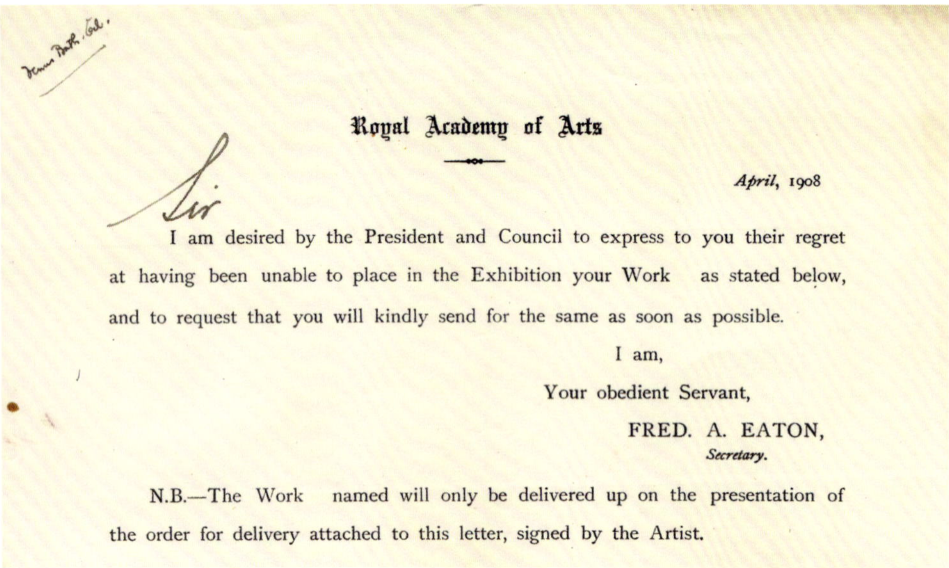

Royal Academy of Arts

April, 1908

Sir

I am desired by the President and Council to express to you their regret at having been unable to place in the Exhibition your Work as stated below, and to request that you will kindly send for the same as soon as possible.

I am,

Your obedient Servant,

FRED. A. EATON,

Secretary.

N.B.—The Work named will only be delivered up on the presentation of the order for delivery attached to this letter, signed by the Artist.

1908 Venus Bath rejection

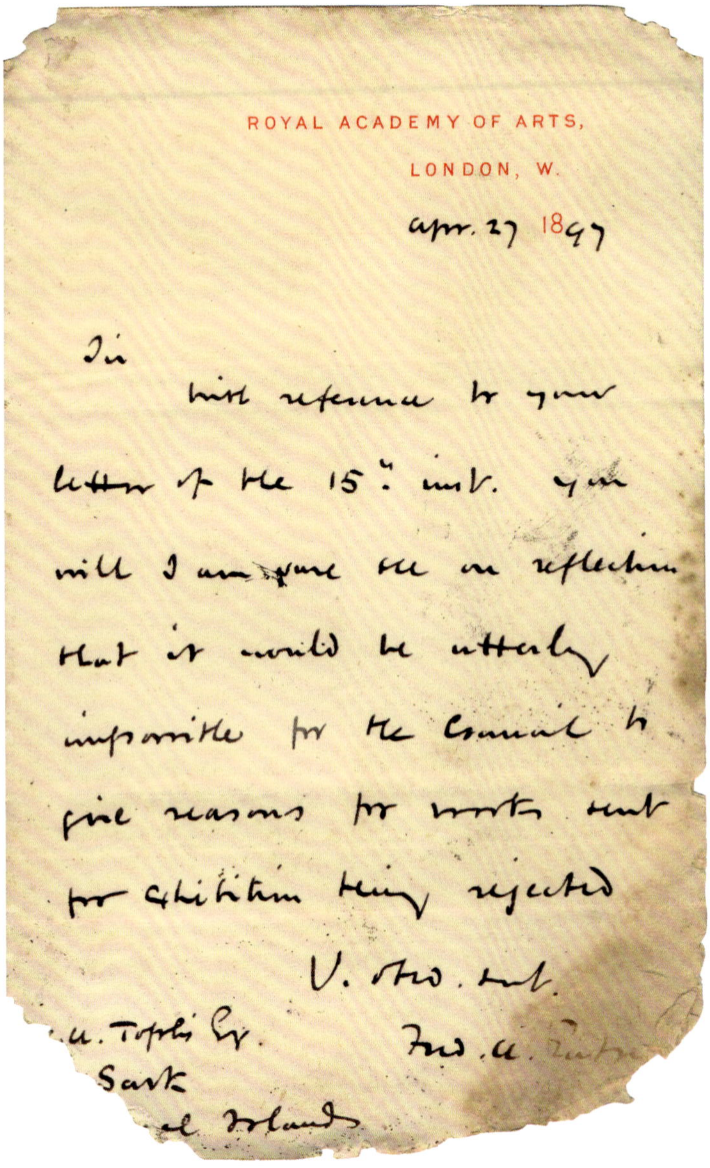

ROYAL ACADEMY OF ARTS,

LONDON, W.

Apr. 27 1897

Sir

With reference to your letter of the 15th inst. you will I am sure see on reflection that it would be utterly impossible for the Council to give reasons for works sent for exhibition being rejected

Y. obed. sert.

…A. Toplis Esq. Fred. A. Eaton

Sark

…l Islands

Earlier letter from the Royal Academy in reply to one from Toplis seemingly demanding reasons for a previous painting's rejection. It seems he did not enjoy criticism however implied

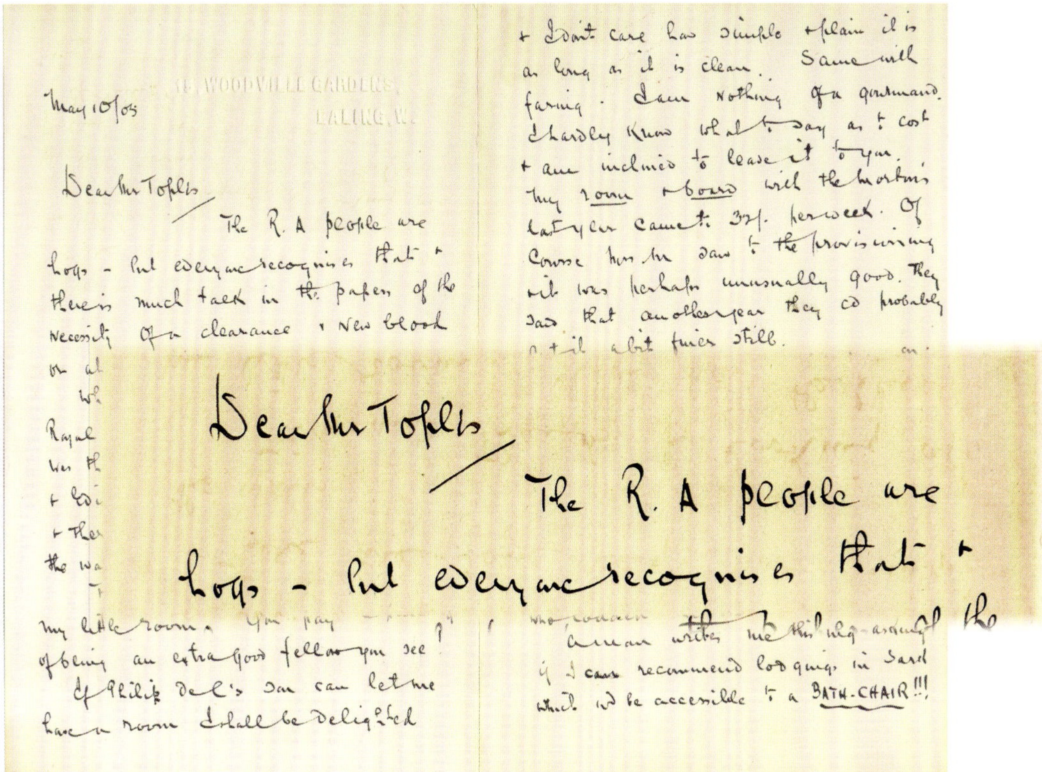
WOODVILLE GARDENS, EALING, W.

May 10/05

Dear Mr Toplis

The R. A people are hogs - but everyone recognises that there is much talk in the papers of the necessity of a clearance & new blood

& I don't care how simple & plain it is as long as it is clean. Same with faring. I am nothing of a gourmand. I hardly know what to say as to cost & am inclined to leave it to you. My room & board with the Martins last year came to 32/- per week. Of course then the days & the provisioning it was perhaps unusually good. They said that another year they cd probably a bit finer still.

my little room. You pay of being an extra good fellow you see? If Philip Del's can let me have a room I shall be delighted

A man writes me this if I can recommend lodgings in Sark which wd be accessible to a BATH-CHAIR!!!

Dear Mr Toplis

The R. A people are hogs - but everyone recognises that &

Letter from Oxenham sympathising with a rejection Toplis suffered from the Royal Academy probably of his Venus Bath picture – '*The R. A people are hogs –*'

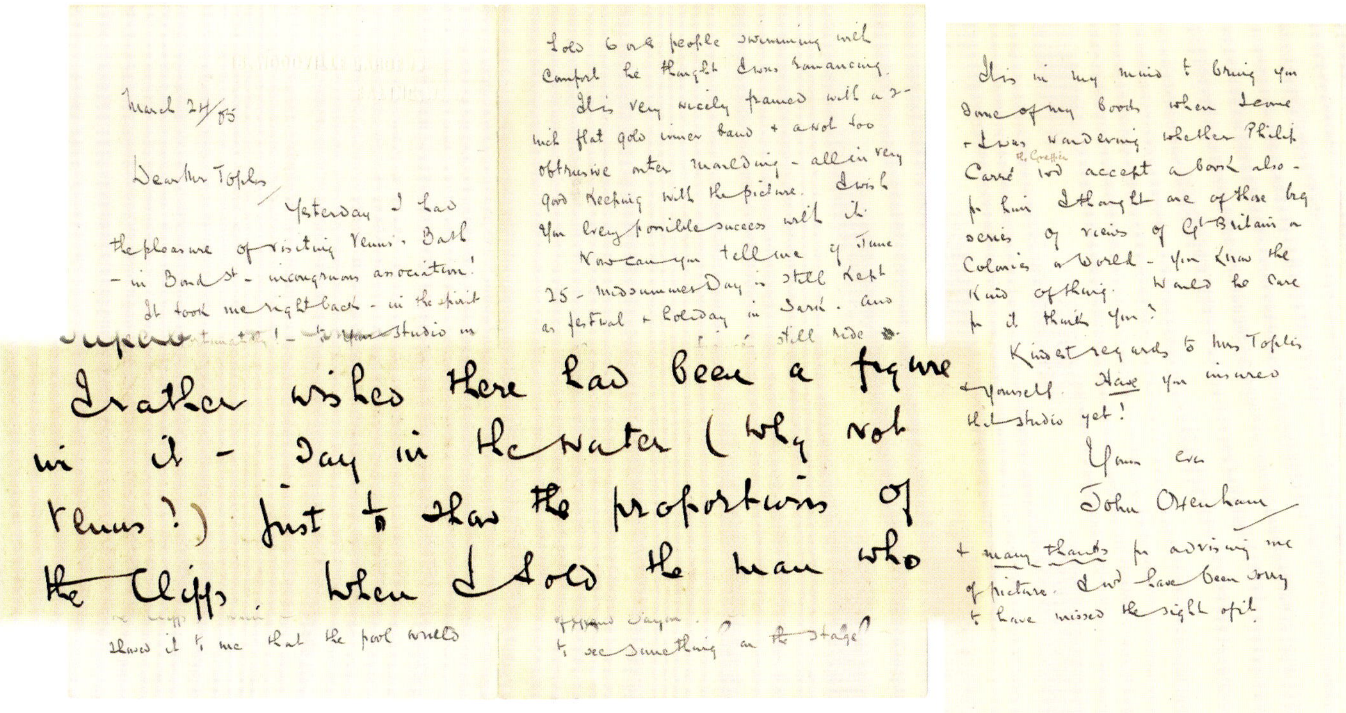
March 24/05

Dear Mr Toplis

Yesterday I had the pleasure of visiting Venus' Bath - in Bond St - incongruous association! It took me right back - in the spirit to your studio in

I rather wishes there had been a figure in it - say in the water (why not Venus?) just to show the proportions of the cliffs. When I told the man who showed it to me that the pool would

told 6 or 8 people swimming with comfort he thought I was romancing. It is very nicely framed with a 2-inch flat gold inner band & a not too obtrusive outer moulding - all in very good keeping with the picture. I wish you every possible success with it. Now can you tell me if June 25 - Midsummer Day is still kept as festival & holiday in Sark. And still

to see something on the stage?

It is in my mind to bring you some of my books when I come & I was wondering whether Philip Carré (R. Greffier) wd accept a book also - for him I thought one of those big series of views of Gt Britain & Colonies & World - you know the kind of thing. Would he care for it think you?

Kindest regards to Mrs Toplis & yourself. Have you insured the studio yet!

Yours ever

John Oxenham

& many thanks for advising me of picture. I wd have been sorry to have missed the sight of it.

Another letter from Oxenham from 1905 referring to The Venus Bath picture and noting: '*I rather wish there had been a figure in it – say in the water (why not Venus?) just to show the proportion of the cliffs.*' so it seems he had an opinion as well as Feeney

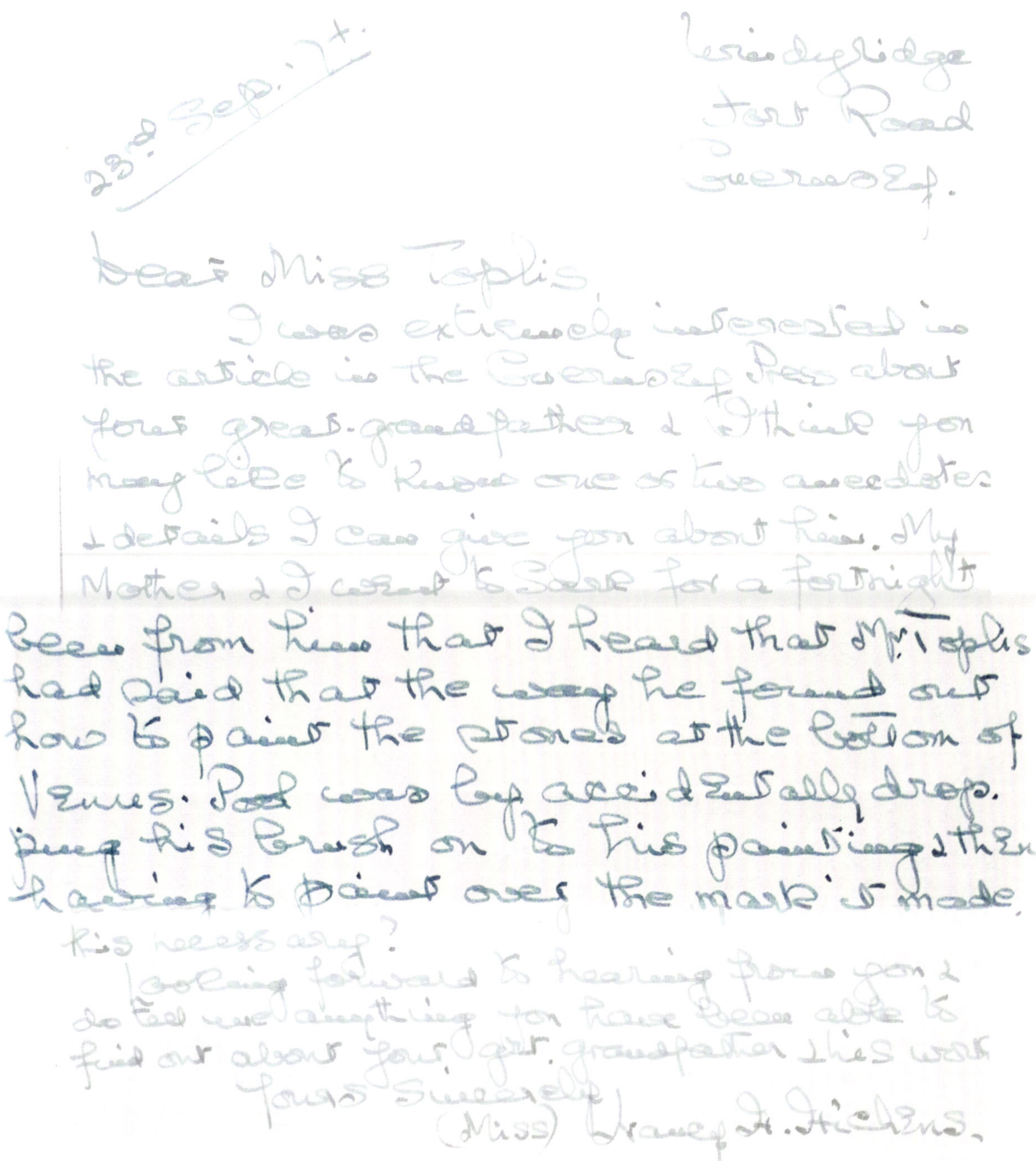

23rd Sep. 7[illegible]

[illegible] Ridge
Fort Road
Guernsey.

Dear Miss Toplis,
I was extremely interested in the article in the Guernsey Press about your great-grandfather & I think you may like to know one or two anecdotes & details I can give you about him. My Mother & I went to Sark for a fortnight

been from him that I heard that Mr Toplis had said that the way he found out how to paint the stones at the bottom of Venus Pool was by accidentally dropping his brush on to his painting & then having to paint over the mark it made.
his [illegible]?
Looking forward to hearing from you & do tell me anything you have been able to find out about your grt. grandfather & his work
Yours sincerely
(Miss) [illegible] H. Hitchins.

Letter to Fiona Toplis from a Miss Hitchins of Guernsey. Top of the back page gives further insight into Toplis' way of working; *'I heard that Mr. Toplis had said that the way he found out how to paint the stones at the bottom of Venus Pool was by accidentally dropping his brush on to his painting and then having to paint over the mark it made'*

The Venus Bath print as it appeared in the 1908 *Book of Sark*

The Later Years

Toplis continued to paint the landscape of Sark into his 70s. In 1930, at the age of seventy-three, he had his final success at the Royal Academy with an old reworked water colour of Les Autelets. That same year, he also submitted an oil painting of Grève de la Ville which was rejected.

Toplis became more and more disillusioned by the changes in tastes in art and did not understand what he referred to as '*the modern school of painters*'. He criticised their work, saying, '*There is too much slackness, too little detail, too much pretence and too little truth!*'

In his latter years, not only was his style of painting falling out of popular favour, but he was finding it increasingly difficult to get to the locations he wished to paint. To further add to his sense of isolation and perhaps alienation, he suffered from increasing deafness to which he would not admit and accused those around him of deliberately tormenting him which caused him to often refuse to see visitors or to interact with those who did come to his home or studio. For several years, vision problems made it difficult for him to do the detailed paintings that defined his unique style, and it was due only to the kindness of an eye doctor who admired his work that his vision was saved.

It appears that he almost completely stopped painting in the final decade of his life. The German Occupation of the Channel Islands brought hardship to all in Sark, and in 1942, Toplis died at the age of eighty-five.

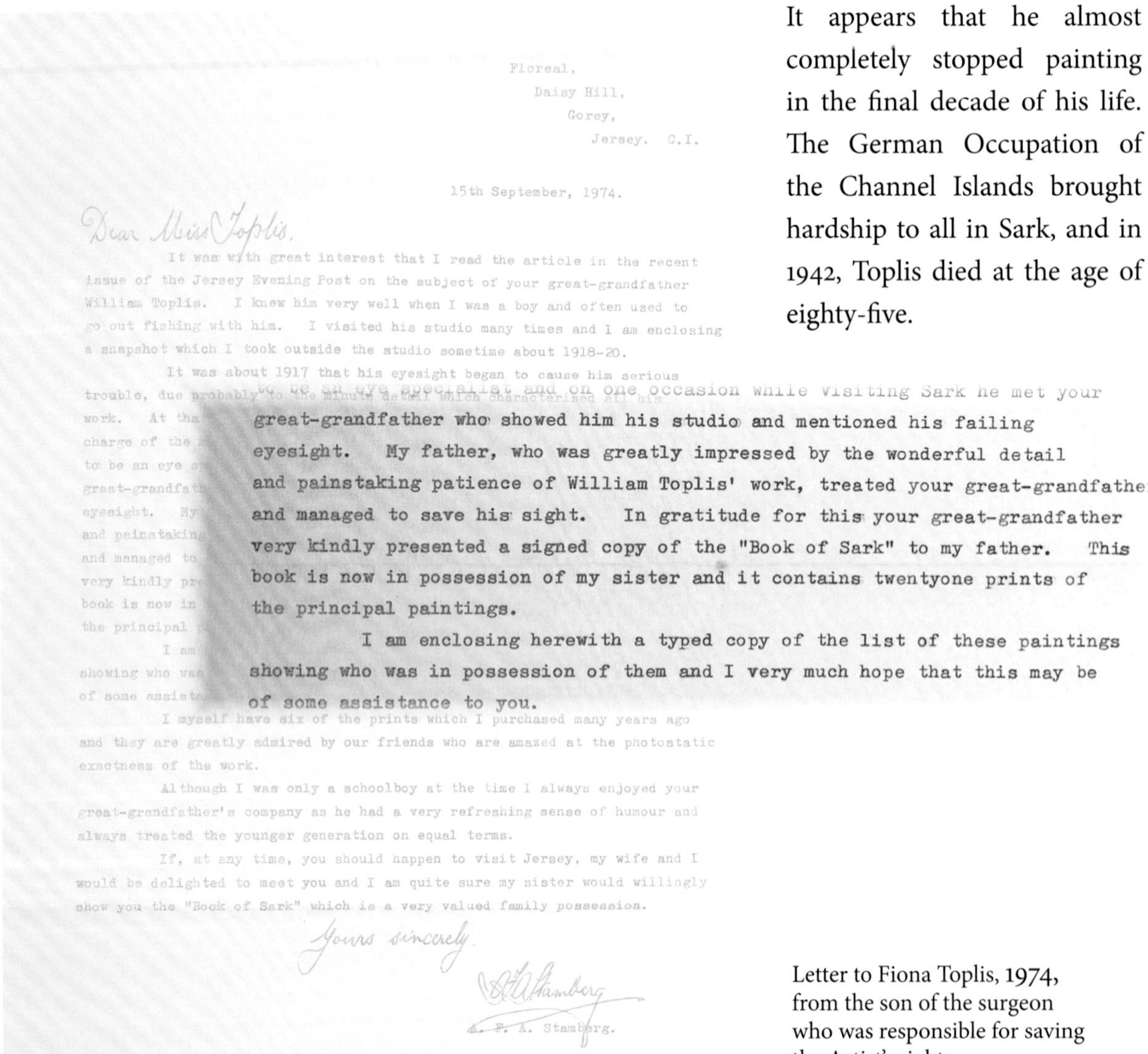

Floreal,
Daisy Hill,
Gorey,
Jersey. C.I.

15th September, 1974.

Dear Miss Toplis,

It was with great interest that I read the article in the recent issue of the Jersey Evening Post on the subject of your great-grandfather William Toplis. I knew him very well when I was a boy and often used to go out fishing with him. I visited his studio many times and I am enclosing a snapshot which I took outside the studio sometime about 1918-20.

It was about 1917 that his eyesight began to cause him serious trouble, due probably to the minute detail which characterised all his work.

to be an eye specialist and on one occasion while visiting Sark he met your great-grandfather who showed him his studio and mentioned his failing eyesight. My father, who was greatly impressed by the wonderful detail and painstaking patience of William Toplis' work, treated your great-grandfather and managed to save his sight. In gratitude for this your great-grandfather very kindly presented a signed copy of the "Book of Sark" to my father. This book is now in possession of my sister and it contains twentyone prints of the principal paintings.

I am enclosing herewith a typed copy of the list of these paintings showing who was in possession of them and I very much hope that this may be of some assistance to you.

I myself have six of the prints which I purchased many years ago and they are greatly admired by our friends who are amazed at the photostatic exactness of the work.

Although I was only a schoolboy at the time I always enjoyed your great-grandfather's company as he had a very refreshing sense of humour and always treated the younger generation on equal terms.

If, at any time, you should happen to visit Jersey, my wife and I would be delighted to meet you and I am quite sure my sister would willingly show you the "Book of Sark" which is a very valued family possession.

Yours sincerely,

A. F. A. Stamberg.

Letter to Fiona Toplis, 1974, from the son of the surgeon who was responsible for saving the Artist's sight

—OFFICE OF—

THE KOOTENAY MINING AND SMELTING CO.

Pilot Bay, B. C., Dec 10 1895

THIS CERTIFIES that the sample of ore said to be from Island of Little Sark assayed for Mr. Toplis.

gave the following result per ton:

No.	MARKS.	Gold. Ounces.	Silver. Ounces.	Lead. Per cent.	Copper. Per cent.	Iron. Per cent.	Silica. Per cent.	Zinc. Per cent.	Mang. Per cent.	Lime. Per cent.	Sulphur Per cent.	Baryta. Per cent.	H_2O. Per cent.
	R. Herrick	—	113.2	56									

113.2 oz silver and 112 lbs. lead to the ton — below surface ore value probably improves — R.D.H.

[illegible] ASSAYER.

Toplis was also interested in silver mining and this slip shows his having sent samples for assay. It caused friction with the then Seigneur as the latter claimed all mineral and mining rights to the Island. Toplis even tried to buy Brecqhou, possibly where this sample came from, but was unsuccessful on no less than three occasions. It is doubtful that he had the resources to exploit any silver but subsequent purchasers of the Island may yet discover if his interest was justified

Toplis

MR. W. A. TOPLIS AND THE ROYAL ACADEMY.

Although eight thousand pictures have been rejected by the Royal Academy Judges, either from want of space or from want of talent on the part of the artists, Sark is well represented by a truly beautiful picture, by Mr. W. A. Toplis, of "La Cave de la Fontaine." It represents a lovely fern cave in La Fontaine Bay, with all the marvellous colouring so familiar to the artistic visitors to these islands. Although the last picture Mr. Toplis exhibited was hung in a splendid position on the line and was afterwards sold to the Marquis of Bute for a large sum, this year's picture is pronounced by Art critics to far excel it in real work, and will no doubt fetch a very high price. Mail & Telegraph - Mar 2nd 93.

Article in *The Telegraph* praising Toplis' work and noting a wealthy collector. The Marquis of Bute's family still owns two Toplis original paintings and when they were viewed in comparison to the modern prints it was seen that the new printing from the plates was a great improvement in quality over the 1908 edition of *The Book of Sark*

Section 2
The First Edition

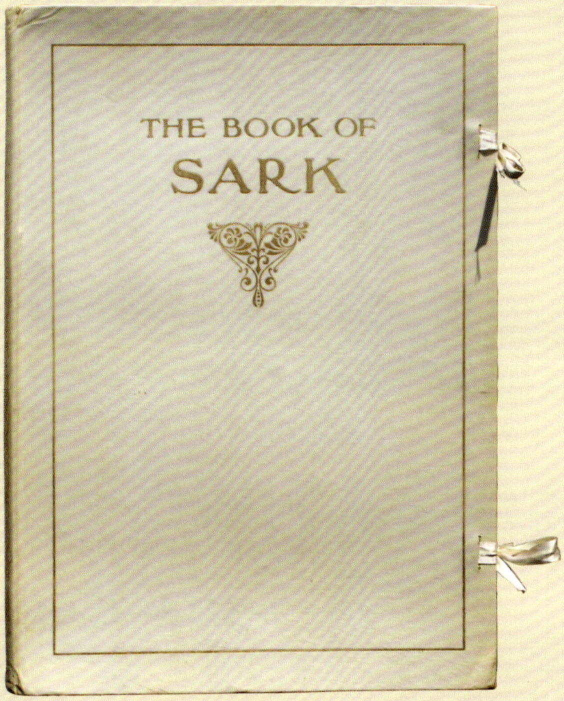

The Original *Book of Sark*

In 1907, Toplis had two paintings accepted for the Royal Academy Exhibition, 'Port Gouray, Sark' and 'In the Port du Moulin'. By that time, fifteen paintings of his had been accepted for Royal Academy Exhibitions and he was a well-known and respected artist. That same year, William Arthur Dunkerley, a writer known by the pseudonym, John Oxenham, proposed to Toplis that he publish a book of colour prints of his best-known works and Oxenham set about trying to help Toplis in this endeavour.

The book would contain reproductions of twenty-one of Toplis' paintings, ten of which had been shown at The Royal Academy. It was agreed that Oxenham would write the descriptive text to accompany the colour plates. He further suggested that two additional articles, one on the geology and one on the flora and fauna of the Island be included. He contacted geologist T G Bonney, asking him to provide a chapter on the geology of Sark, and botanist E D Marquand to provide a chapter on the flora and fauna of Sark. Both men agreed and their reward was set at one copy of the book each. Oxenham was to receive three copies for his contribution and Toplis would receive six copies plus twenty percent royalties on the rest.

The book would measure eighteen by thirteen inches. The pictures would be cut flush and mounted on black paper, fastened at the top only to minimize the possibility of creasing. Each mount would bear the signature of the artist and the picture would be protected with an interleaf of fine tissue paper bearing the title of the painting. The book would either be bound in vellum or cloth and boxed.

Oxenham contacted publishers Hodder & Stoughton and a meeting was arranged between Toplis and a Mr. Williams of the publishing house in May 1907. Hodder & Stoughton were not enthusiastic about taking on this project and Mr. Williams later wrote to Oxenham voicing his trepidation about it:

'I am frankly, very afraid of colour books, and I have my doubts as to the possible sale of one on Sark. The whole colour book idea has been overdone. Whether a portfolio of these pictures would sell is another matter. It all depends upon what Toplis would want for his rights in reproduction. I think some of his pictures are really beautiful, at the same time I am not bowled over by them in the bulk.'
(See reproduction of this letter on page 35)

Despite their initial concern, Hodder & Stoughton agreed to publish five hundred individually numbered and signed copies to be signed by the artist and author plus twenty unnumbered copies for library deposits and the customary gratis copies for authors and contributors. They agreed to publish on condition that Toplis find three hundred subscribers at three guineas each before the end of the year. This was a very expensive book for that period and Toplis wrote to everyone he could think of who might have the means or interest to purchase the book. Subscriptions, however, were slow to come in and by October, only one hundred and fifty completed forms had been received.

In August 1907, Toplis allowed himself to be influenced by friends who knew nothing about publishing and he wrote to the publishers with a list of demands that almost ended the project. These demands were punctuated with a threat to change publishers, something that Hodder & Stoughton might have been glad to accept and would have done so had it not been for Oxenham's negotiating skills. Oxenham convinced them to ignore Toplis' demands and continue with the project. He was, in fact,

The most telling photograph illustrating why Toplis was dissatisfied with the proofs and printing of his book.
The large picture in the middle is the Sark copy of the original painting (The Fairy Grotto), the print on the bottom left is the new reproduction from the original printing plates and the one top right is in a 1908 *Book of Sark*

able to convince them to publish when the subscription list reached only two hundred, one hundred subscriptions shy of the originally agreed upon number.

A memorandum in Toplis' personal papers indicates that at one point there was a miscommunication between Toplis and Professor Bonney which might have further delayed publication. The first letter, dated October 16, 1907 is an apparent response to an inquiry by Toplis about the chapter on the geology of Sark. Bonney categorically denies any knowledge of such a manuscript or any promise to write one. This is followed by a memorandum from his desk dated November 22, 1907 which reads:

'I am sorry to have troubled you by a stupid mistake. I wrote the chapter as stated and intended to post it, then kept it back to look up a small detail and fell under the delusion that I had, as originally intended, posted it. This evening going to the receptacle, where things on the wheel are kept, for something else I found the manuscript. Pray forgive me. I do not often, even now, make such blunders. T. G. Bonney.'

While only one hundred and fifty subscriptions had been received, Toplis managed to make up the additional fifty subscriptions by agreeing to take forty copies himself with Oxenham taking ten. At that point, Hodders instructed the printers to begin the printing process. The text pages of the book were printed by the well known printers Unwin Bros Ltd. of Woking, the colour plates were produced by Messrs Carl Hentschel. (Carl Hentschel himself, as well as being one of the foremost colour plate producers of the time, appeared in the classic English comic novel by Jerome K Jerome – *Three Men in a Boat* – where he was known as 'Harris')

Colour proofs of the pictures were continually being sent to Toplis but he was never satisfied. Finally in January 1908, he was given an ultimatum by Hodder & Stoughton and he grudgingly stopped complaining about the print quality. Note: When looking at the new prints made from the original plates, we were pleased to see that the reproduction of the new prints is much closer to the colours, contrast and detail in the original paintings that we have been able to view. The prints in the original *Book of Sark* had more red and ochre tones than did the original paintings, and we surmise that it was this that Toplis found objectionable in the original prints. Colour printing techniques have greatly advanced since the early 1900s and we believe that Toplis might have been far more satisfied with *The Book of Sark Centenary Edition* proofs.

In addition to the colour reproduction complaints, Toplis also decided that he wanted the pictures to have white margins, but he was informed that:

'The pictures are being cut flush as arranged when you were here. It is too late now to leave white margins. As we have informed you more than once we have decided not to print any gold borders, for we are emphatically of the opinion that the plates are more artistic and more interesting if inserted in accordance with our original agreement. We have gone to some considerable additional expense beyond that originally contemplated and on this head alone we are unable to incur the further expense involved.

There is far more liability of creasing the plates if they are fastened all round, and the leaf of the book is so large and strong that there is no probability of creasing, especially as the prints are further protected by the thin title leaf. The plates we fear would be likely to be injured if an attempt were made to fasten them all round.

As you know, we are always most anxious to carry out your wishes, and if we are unable to do so in these matters we hope you will believe our decision is made entirely in the interests of the book and in the light of our experience and of others who issue similar art publications.'

Though the 1908 *Book of Sark* is a handsome volume few copies survive in very good condition. The materials used were not all of archival quality and the text paper is often discoloured and stained, and the black mounting paper incredibly fragile and broken.

A page from the 1908 *Book of Sark* with, below, mounted prints – possibly proofs – that accompanied Book 'Number 369' and was given by Toplis to his daughter Irenée in 1914.
The prints show a progression of colouring and though Toplis may not have been happy with his proofs it did not stop him mounting and signing them, as here, presumably for sale

Documents Relating to the 1908 Publication:

Telegrams:
Expositor London.
Telephones:
3068 Central,
920 Holborn (Advt. Dept.)

JEHW/EC

St. Paul's House,
Warwick Square,
London, E.C., Aug.8th/07

W. Toplis Esq.,
56 Ritherdon Road,
Balham, S.W.

Dear Mr. Toplis,

We have heard from Mr. Oxenham that you have received the prospectuses of the Book of Sark safely, and we regret that they were sent by rail and so caused delay.

In order that there may be no misunderstanding we now put into writing the terms agreed upon for the publication of the book, viz.,

1. We are only to publish the book conditionally upon your obtaining 300 subscribers at Three Guineas by the end of December of this year.

2. That we pay you 20% royalty upon the published price of all copies sold, the accounts to be made up annually at our stocktaking March 31st.

3. That you are to receive six gratis copies on publication.

Yours very faithfully,
Hodder & Stoughton

The agreement between Toplis and his publishers, sent to a London address

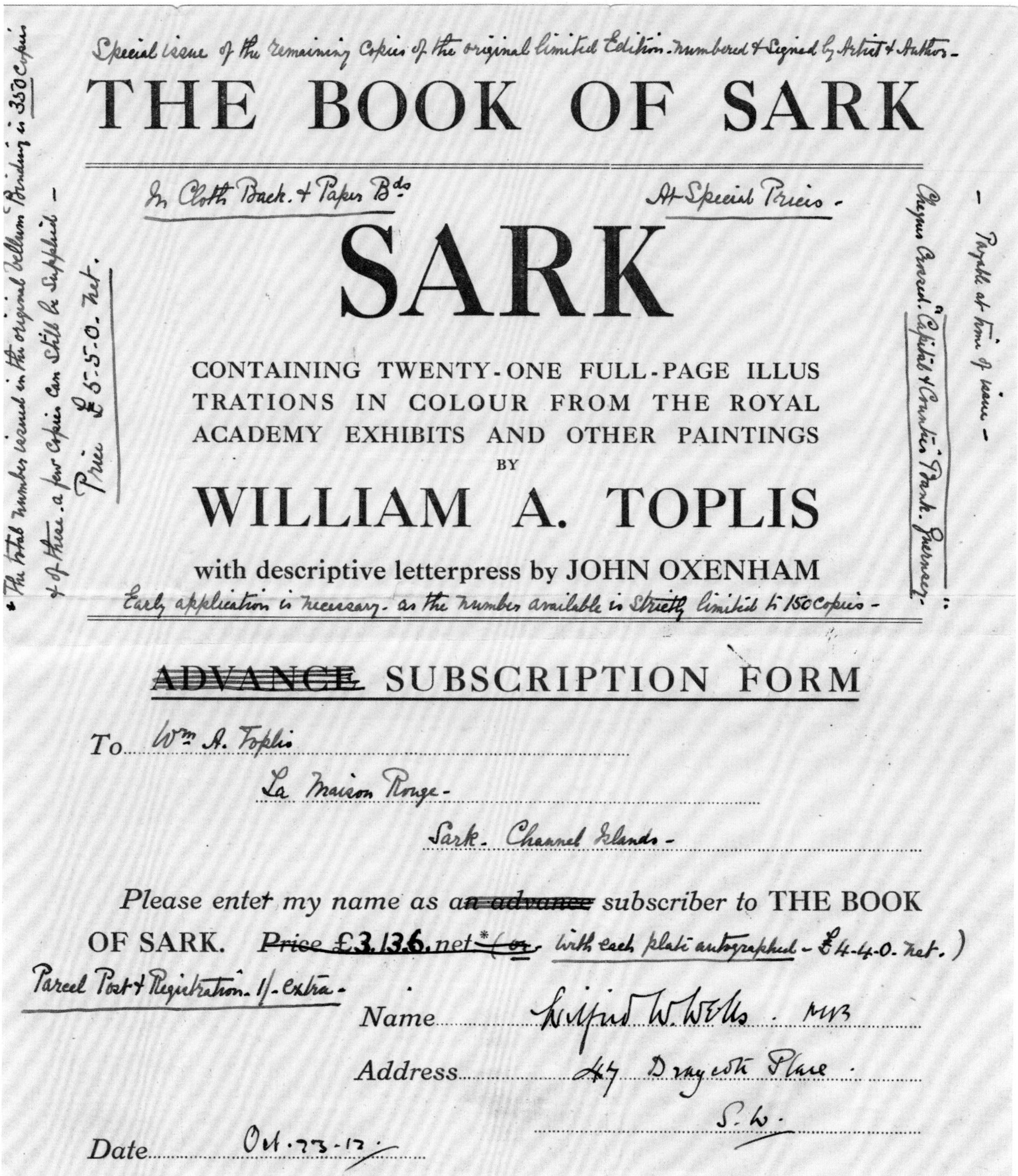

Special issue of the remaining copies of the original limited Edition. numbered & signed by Artist & Author.

THE BOOK OF SARK

In Cloth Back & Paper Bds. At Special Prices.

SARK

CONTAINING TWENTY-ONE FULL-PAGE ILLUSTRATIONS IN COLOUR FROM THE ROYAL ACADEMY EXHIBITS AND OTHER PAINTINGS BY

WILLIAM A. TOPLIS

with descriptive letterpress by JOHN OXENHAM

Early application is necessary. as the number available is strictly limited to 150 copies.

* The total number issued in the original Vellum Binding is 350 copies & of these. a few copies can still be supplied – Price £5-5-0. net.

– Payable at time of issue – Cheques crossed "Capital & Counties Bank. Guernsey".

~~ADVANCE~~ SUBSCRIPTION FORM

To Wm. A. Toplis
La Maison Rouge.
Sark. Channel Islands.

Please enter my name as ~~an advance~~ subscriber to THE BOOK OF SARK. ~~Price £3.13.6. net*~~ ~~(or~~ with each plate autographed – £4-4-0. net.)

Parcel Post & Registration. 1/- extra.

Name Wilfred W. Wells. MB

Address 47 Draycott Place. S.W.

Date Oct. 23-17.

Successful order, annotated by Toplis and showing an increased price over the 'advance' subscription price of three guineas

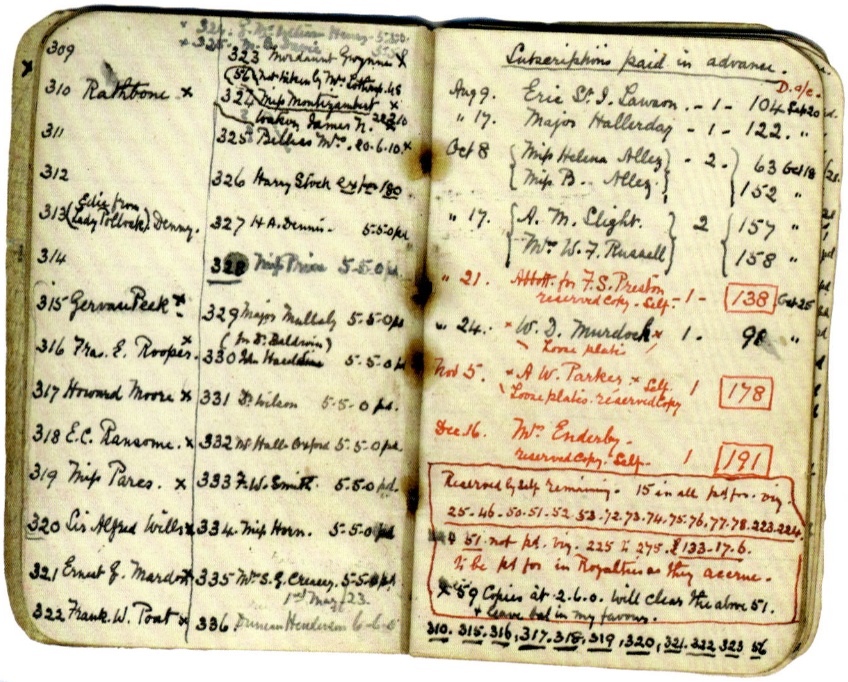

Toplis' notebook showing subscriptions received and some comments from him. This is actual size

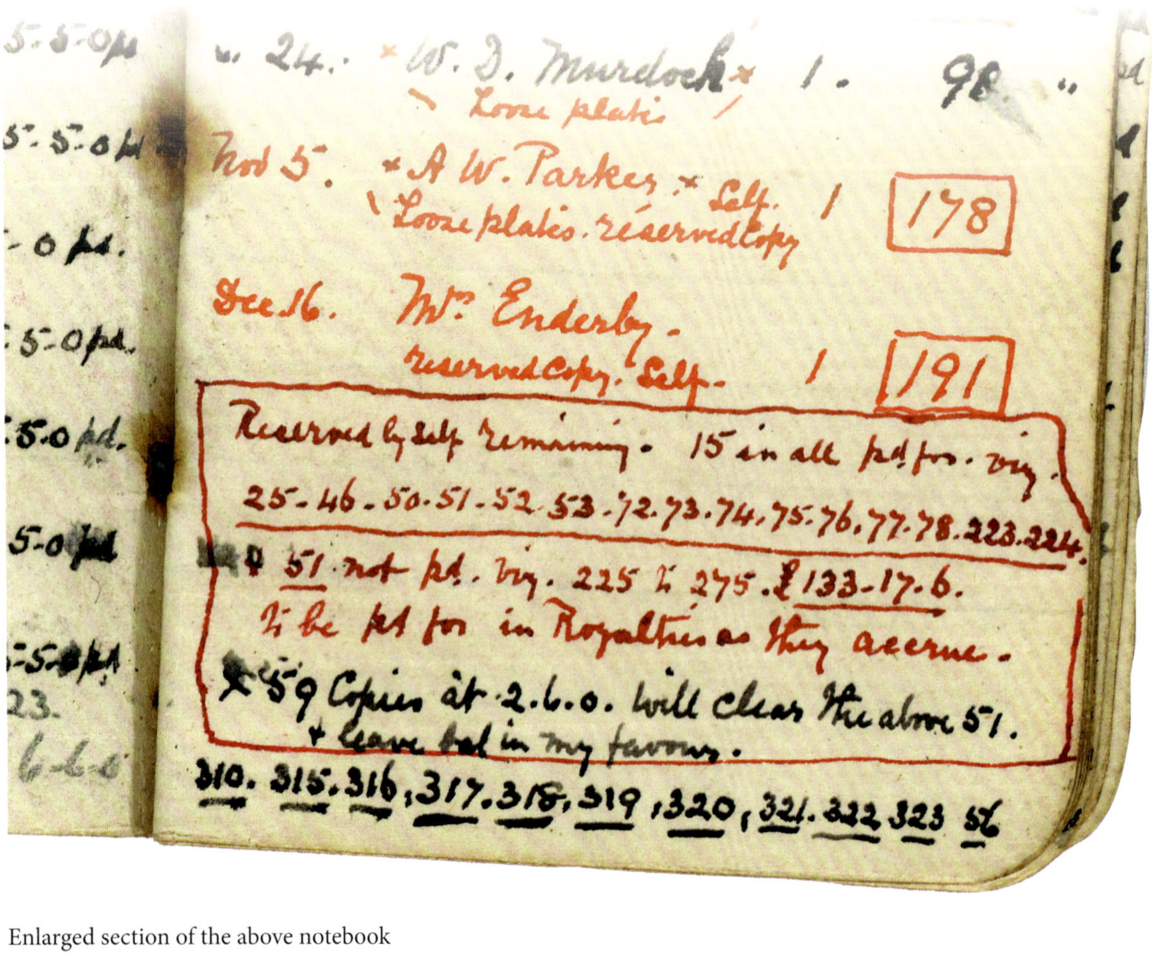

Enlarged section of the above notebook

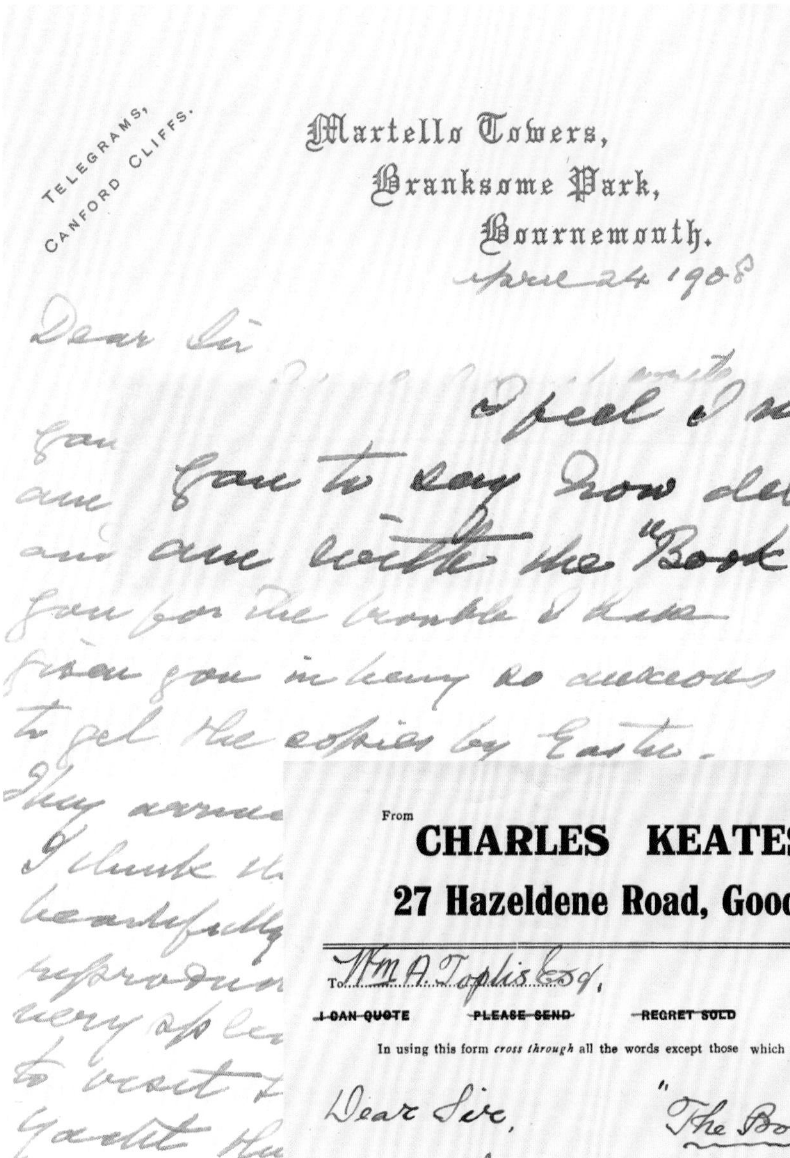

TELEGRAMS, CANFORD CLIFFS.

Martello Towers,
Branksome Park,
Bournemouth.
April 24 1908

Dear Sir

I feel I must write you to say how delighted I am with the "Book of Sark"

you for the trouble I have
from you in being so anxious
to get the copies by Easter.
They arrive
I think th
beautifully
reproduc
very appl
to visit
Yacht the

A note from a happy customer on reciept of his *Book of Sark* in 1908

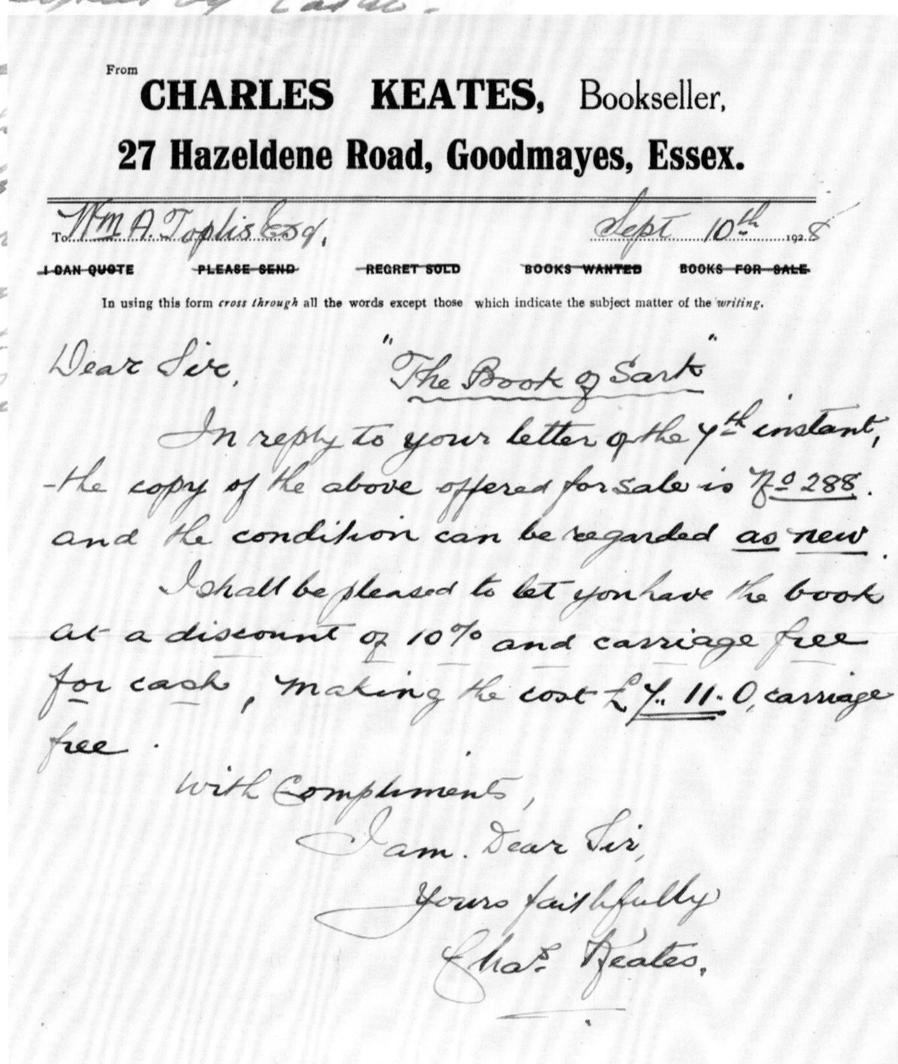

From
CHARLES KEATES, Bookseller,
27 Hazeldene Road, Goodmayes, Essex.

To Wm A. Toplis Esq. Sept 10th 1928

~~I CAN QUOTE~~ ~~PLEASE SEND~~ ~~REGRET SOLD~~ ~~BOOKS WANTED~~ ~~BOOKS FOR SALE~~

In using this form *cross through* all the words except those which indicate the subject matter of the *writing*.

Dear Sir, "The Book of Sark"

In reply to your letter of the 7th instant, the copy of the above offered for sale is No 288. and the condition can be regarded as new.

I shall be pleased to let you have the book at a discount of 10% and carriage free for cash, making the cost £7. 11. 0, carriage free.

With Compliments,
I am. Dear Sir,
Yours faithfully
Chas. Keates.

Toplis buying a *Book of Sark* back from a dealer, presumably because he had a personal customer or wished to make use of the plates. It shows a significant increase in the value of *The Book of Sark* shortly after publication

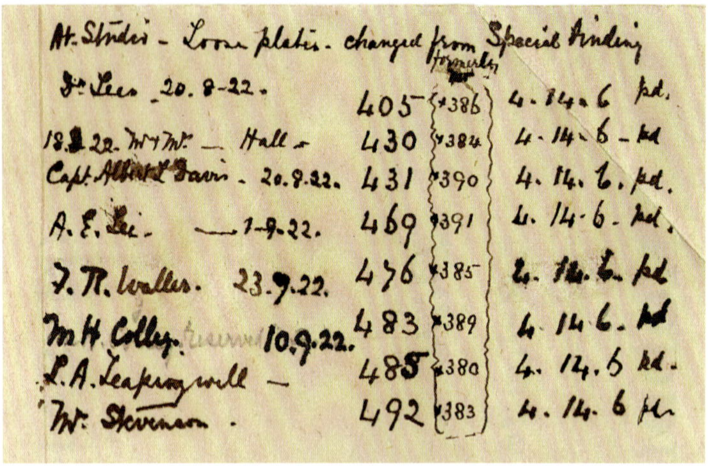

At Studio – Loose plates – changed from Special Binding

[illegible]	20.8.22.	405	386	4. 14. 6 pd.
[illegible]		430	384	4. 14. 6 – pd
Capt. [illegible]	20.9.22.	431	390	4. 14. 6. pd.
A. E. [illegible]	1.9.22.	469	391	4. 14. 6. pd.
[illegible]	23.9.22.	476	385	4. 14. 6. pd
M H Colley	10.9.22.	483	389	4. 14. 6. pd
[illegible]		485	380	4. 14. 6 pd.
[illegible]		492	383	4. 14. 6 pd

A note in one of the Toplis notebooks indicating that some of the special binding edition were either split up for individual plate sales or rebound and renumbered

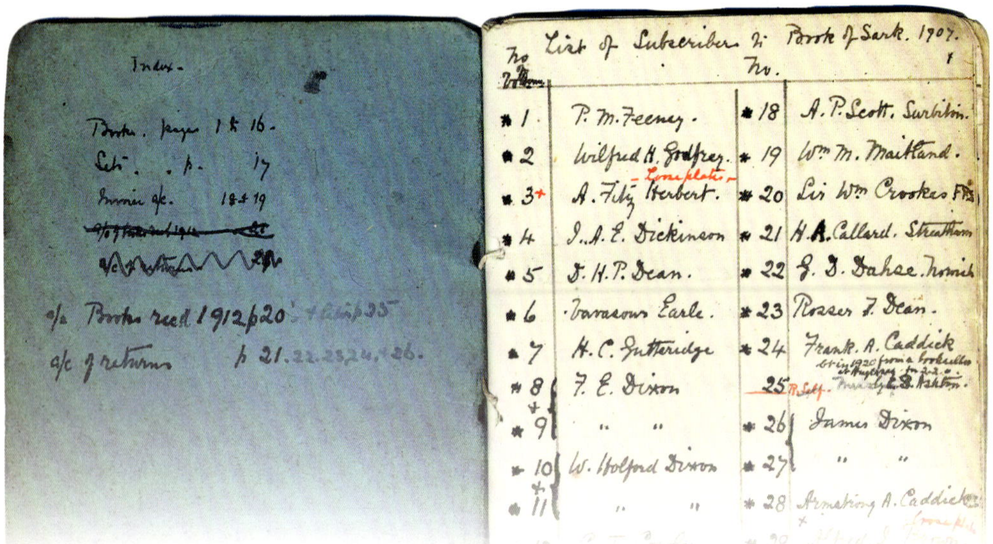

List of Subscribers to Book of Sark. 1907.

Notebook listing subscribers, this page showing the first 31 to receive *The Book of Sark*

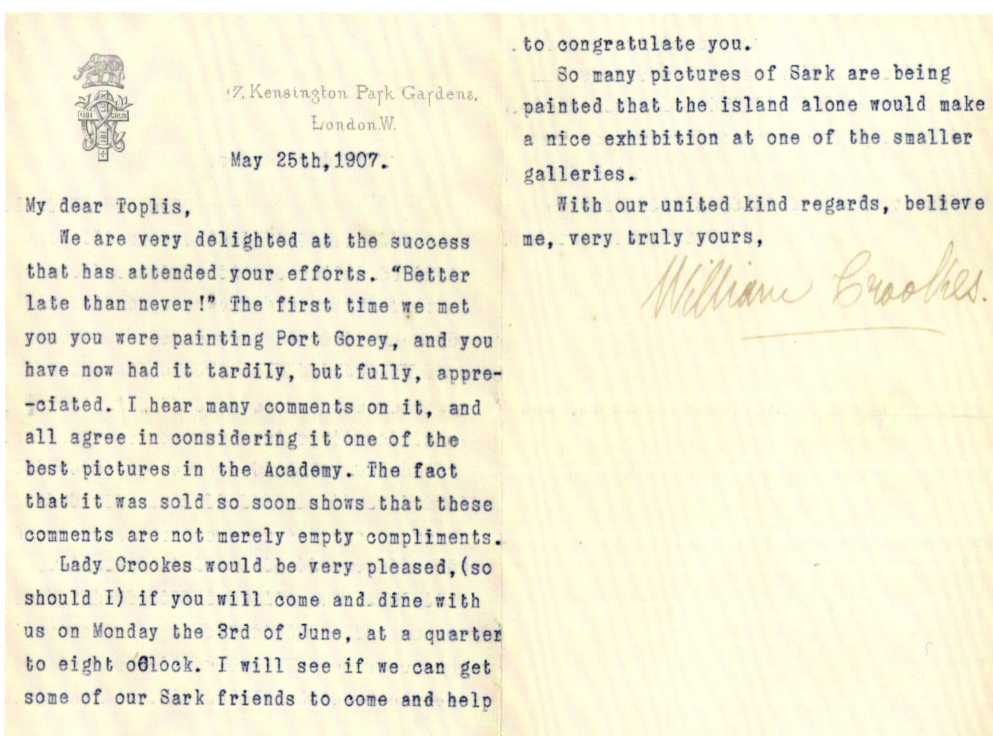

7, Kensington Park Gardens,
London.W.

May 25th,1907.

My dear Toplis,

We are very delighted at the success that has attended your efforts. "Better late than never!" The first time we met you you were painting Port Gorey, and you have now had it tardily, but fully, appre--ciated. I hear many comments on it, and all agree in considering it one of the best pictures in the Academy. The fact that it was sold so soon shows that these comments are not merely empty compliments.

Lady Crookes would be very pleased,(so should I) if you will come and dine with us on Monday the 3rd of June, at a quarter to eight o'Clock. I will see if we can get some of our Sark friends to come and help to congratulate you.

So many pictures of Sark are being painted that the island alone would make a nice exhibition at one of the smaller galleries.

With our united kind regards, believe me, very truly yours,

William Crookes.

(Sir) William Crookes – a collector of Toplis' paintings

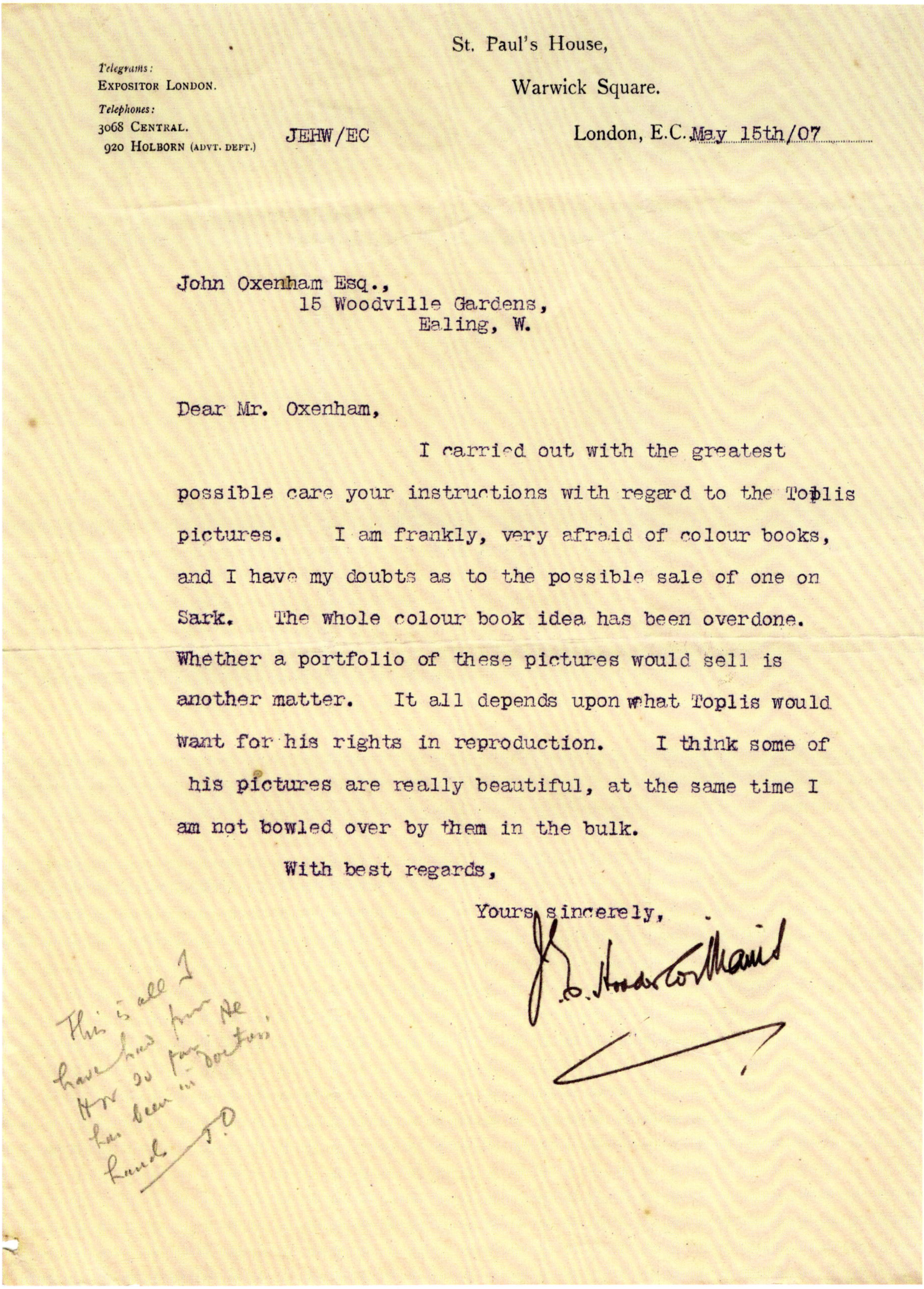

Telegrams:
EXPOSITOR LONDON.
Telephones:
3068 CENTRAL.
920 HOLBORN (ADVT. DEPT.)

St. Paul's House,
Warwick Square.

JEHW/EC

London, E.C. May 15th/07

John Oxenham Esq.,
15 Woodville Gardens,
Ealing, W.

Dear Mr. Oxenham,

I carried out with the greatest possible care your instructions with regard to the Toplis pictures. I am frankly, very afraid of colour books, and I have my doubts as to the possible sale of one on Sark. The whole colour book idea has been overdone. Whether a portfolio of these pictures would sell is another matter. It all depends upon what Toplis would want for his rights in reproduction. I think some of his pictures are really beautiful, at the same time I am not bowled over by them in the bulk.

With best regards,

Yours sincerely,

J. E. Hodder Williams

This is all I have had from the H S so far has been in Doctor's hands J.O.

A less than encouraging letter from the potential publisher of *The Book of Sark*

Section 3
Producing the Centenary Edition

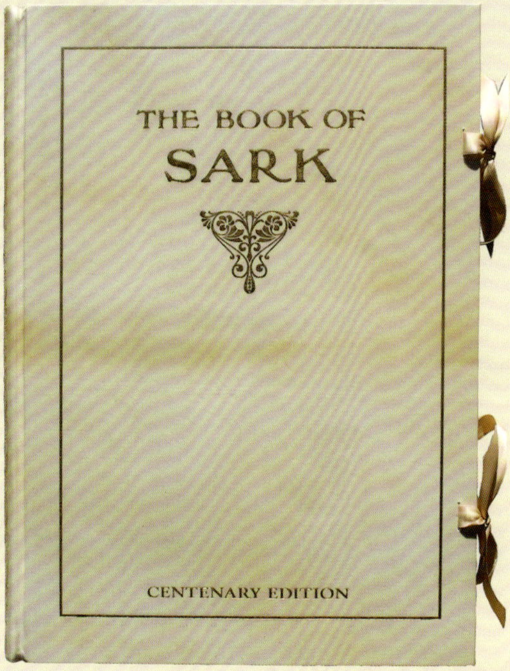

Notes on Publishing the Centenary Edition

It was on the visit to St Cuthbert's Paper Mill in Somerset that the unique nature of this project really became clear. After a long meeting to review the specifications of the paper to be made and a tour of the mill, the proprietor was explaining about the paper making machine that would be used and casually dropped its year of manufacture into his description – 1908.

1908! This was the year Oxenham and Toplis achieved publication of the original *Book of Sark* – and now a special making of an archive paper for the *Centenary Edition* was being discussed and it was to be made on a machine manufactured and installed in the mill in the same year. Add this to the fact that the text is typeset to exactly match the original, the binding is of English Vellum with 22ct Gold tooling and the prints are to be produced using the original 100 year old halftone copper printing plates! There is unlikely to be another publication like this in the United Kingdom and probably the world.

A truly unique project.

The Start

The real beginning of this project was the meeting with a Toplis direct descendant, Fiona Kelly (née Toplis) who owns the original printing plates for the colour illustrations from *The Book of Sark*. An initial visit to the Oxford Fine Press Book Fair in November 2007 found a printer who was able and willing to produce a proof from one of the plate sets of red, yellow and blue. Colour printing originally used only three colour plates, around the time of the original *Book of Sark's* production a fourth plate for black printing, was introduced and the system we use today developed.

The proof showed the plates to be in fine condition with only a few minor marks. It was decided to accept the marks on the plates as an inevitable consequence of using original 100 year old copper plates. The final printed results are immeasurably better than could have been expected and reinforce the authenticity of the publication. It took a considerable length of time for all the aspects of production, plate printing, text printing, materials, finishing and binding to be examined, reviewed for practicality and eventually costed but by September 2008 the details had been agreed and the production was as follows.

Production

The colour plates have been reproduced at the Logan Press on a 50 year old Heidelberg cylinder printing machine operated by Brian Watkin, a trained letterpress printer with over 40 years experience. He is one of the last to undergo the full seven year apprenticeship for letterpress colour printing.

An exact copy of the text was set on a Monotype caster and with handset titles, both by Stan Lane at Gloucester Typesetting. The fount is as the original – Caslon – with occasional additions of decorative alternatives where the 1908 edition indicated. All type was cast from 'Hot Metal' and the text pages printed by John Grice at Evergreen Press.

Prints were mounted and tissue overlays tipped in by Betty Roberts who also sewed the individual page sections at The Fine Book Bindery in Wellingborough. The book block made of the component parts was then sent to Derry's for hand binding in either English Vellum or Buckram with 22ct Gold tooling on front and spine, gilding the heads of the text pages, Vellum edition closed by two silk ties. Derry's were chosen having already restored several copies of the 1908 *Book of Sark* and their quality and attention to detail were very much appreciated.

The Book of Sark Centenary Edition and this accompanying volume are presented in a cloth bound Solander Box which is finished with a leather and gold label and made at The Fine Book Bindery. The Solander Box is named after the botanist Daniel Solander, who first created the design of box in the 18th century while working in the British Museum.

Sewing the sections to form the book block

Finished book in the Solander Box

Materials

It was extremely important to find materials that matched those used in the original *Book of Sark* as closely as possible in appearance, and that were of the highest archival quality, in order to produce an aesthetically appealing and above all lasting production – a book including a collection of fine art prints, produced to the highest quality.

The colour prints were produced on acid free calendared paper using light fast inks.

The prints were mounted on an archival quality backing paper – in the few original 1908 volumes still available the backing paper was often very damaged and fragile. In fact, the original books had been made using materials that were not always of the highest quality. This was particularly true of the backing paper, but also the end papers and text papers which have discoloured over time. Gilbert's 'Oxford Smoked' mounting paper that is used in the *The Book of Sark Centenary Edition* for the prints is totally neutral and acid free, it will support and display the Toplis prints without deteriorating. Colour prints and mounting paper are covered with Pergamenata Naturale archival interleaving paper.

The text paper took a little time to organise. After much consideration of colour, weight, bulk, feel and performance, Somerset Satin from St Cuthbert's Paper Mill in Wells, Somerset was chosen. This is a mould made paper, using one of the few remaining cylinder mould machines left in the world. The paper was specially commissioned for this project, of which more later. A first visit to the paper mill reviewed the manufacture, the alternatives, and the timing (also the extraordinary coincidence of 1908). An initial test making gave enough material for a dummy – a fully bound sample of *The Book of Sark Centenary Edition* – to confirm all specifications and appearance.

The paper was made from 100% cotton ensuring the highest archival standards. A vitally important detail is the 'grain direction' of the fibres, to ensure that once bound the book opens easily and pages fall naturally one after the other. This is totally dictated by the grain direction and the printing and binding specifications had to be known in order for the paper to be manufactured correctly. Having visited the mill twice and agreed all specification, approximately 1.5 tonnes of mould made Somerset Satin in 'soft white' colour, milled to 260 microns was produced.

The book block was finished and bound using linings of acid free paper, mill board, acid free reversible glue, English classic Vellum or Buckram and 22ct Gold tooling, to give durability and permanence as well as aesthetic appeal.

Printing the Plates

The initial proofs from a set of plates were produced on a proofing press, which was sufficient to show the plates were still capable of reproduction. But to accurately judge the quality and colour achievable, all 21 plates were proofed on the actual printing machine. This gave an absolute indication of the excellent quality despite using 100 year old originals and gave a finished print which could be reviewed. Printing true to the plates, without excess changes or corrections to usual ink weights gave a lovely result, any expected evidence of the age of the plates could be minimised and in every case where a comparison could be made *The Book of Sark Centenary Edition* prints are closer to the Toplis original paintings than the 1908 reproductions.

Each colour print is made up of 3 colours; red, yellow and blue. There is a plate for each and these are mounted in succession on the printing machine, inked, then the blank paper rolled over the plate surface to transfer the colour. When dry, the process is repeated with the next colour and finally the last to give a finished result. It is a meticulous and lengthy process.

Unwrapping the original plates

Mounting on the 'honeycomb' before locking up the printing machine

Proofing the magenta plate

The Printing Process as Described by Patrick Roe and Brian Watkin, the Printers of the Colour Plates:

A set of plates in original wrappings

'The first thing we needed to do was make up some aluminium backing plates the right thickness to mount the plates on to the Cornerstone Honeycomb mounting material. This is brilliant and very very expensive stuff (a full forme of this for a Heidelberg cylinder costs over £1,000). It is perfect for printing 3 or 4 plates in close register because the "clips" which hold the plates down are minutely adjustable to position the plate anywhere on the Honeycomb forme. Also, when printing on a Heidelberg cylinder, the plates have to be exactly "type-high" (0.917" in the United Kingdom) so that the rollers can make a perfect pass over the plates and also so the impression can be adjusted according to the paper used. When mounting the copper halftones, sometimes modern double sided adhesive sheets did the trick, but where the old plates were slightly bent, having been taken off their original wood mounts years ago, where they had been nailed down, we had to "rivet" down any high areas of the plate. This we did by using the existing nail holes around the edge of the plate and hand drilling through the aluminium backing sheet, then countersinking both sides, pulling through a mounting pin, bending it into the countersink and grinding it off flat.

Then each plate (65 in total) had to be carefully cleaned with a solvent strong enough to remove 100-year-old dried on ink and gentle enough not to attack the surface. We found MRC (meter roller cleaner) was best for this with a soft natural bristle brush. Proofing each set of prints on the Heidelberg cylinder also helped as it meant each plate was cleaned several times. Proofing this way was also essential because we can only see how one colour prints at a time and do not know how the final print will look until the last colour goes on. Each colour has to dry for a day before the next colour can be added. When printing the proofs we kept a copy of every individual colour so that when it came to printing the final prints, we could see what the individual colours looked like and so could adjust if necessary. Not too many proofs needed too much adjustment and it was usually something like "a bit more yellow" or "a bit less red." So we could look at the yellow print from the proof and increase the amount of ink or look at the red print from the proofs and reduce the ink on that pass.

The run of 1,000 lots of 21 pictures involved taking over 80,000 impressions as each colour had to be set up and registered (fitted) with the other colours twice (once for the proof and once for the run).

Then the part which really makes all the difference... makeready. This is the process of constant review and adjustment of the impression to achieve the optimum result. As this is a relief process, the copper halftones have to be inked, really evenly and carefully, then the inked plate pressed onto the paper. For simple jobs using all new type, makeready will be minimal as the type is all the same height and the thicknesses of the lines all similar. However, when there are differences between areas of very pale (or even no image at all) and very solid areas, the makeready has to compensate for this by increasing the impression (pressure) in the solid areas and reducing the impression in the light areas. This is done by tearing pieces of tissue paper and placing them accurately in the packing underneath the solid areas. Some of these plates required a difference of 6 or 7 sheets... torn to avoid any hard edges in tone graduation.

This is so different from offset litho, todays method of printing from a flat plate, where the impression is always the same all over the image. It is not a relief process and the ink is simply transferred from the rubber cylinder because it is wet and not through pressure. However the main difference is of course the fact that the finished result can be seen immediately as modern litho presses are made up of effectively 4 different machines, in line, which print the 4 process colours in one pass of the sheet. At 10,000 sheets per hour and since these pictures could be printed 9 different views per sheet with ease, this would equate to a printing time of about half an hour in total for all the pictures! Letterpress printing these pictures has taken more than 260 hours (7 weeks, full-time non-stop)'.

The Heidelberg cylinder printing press

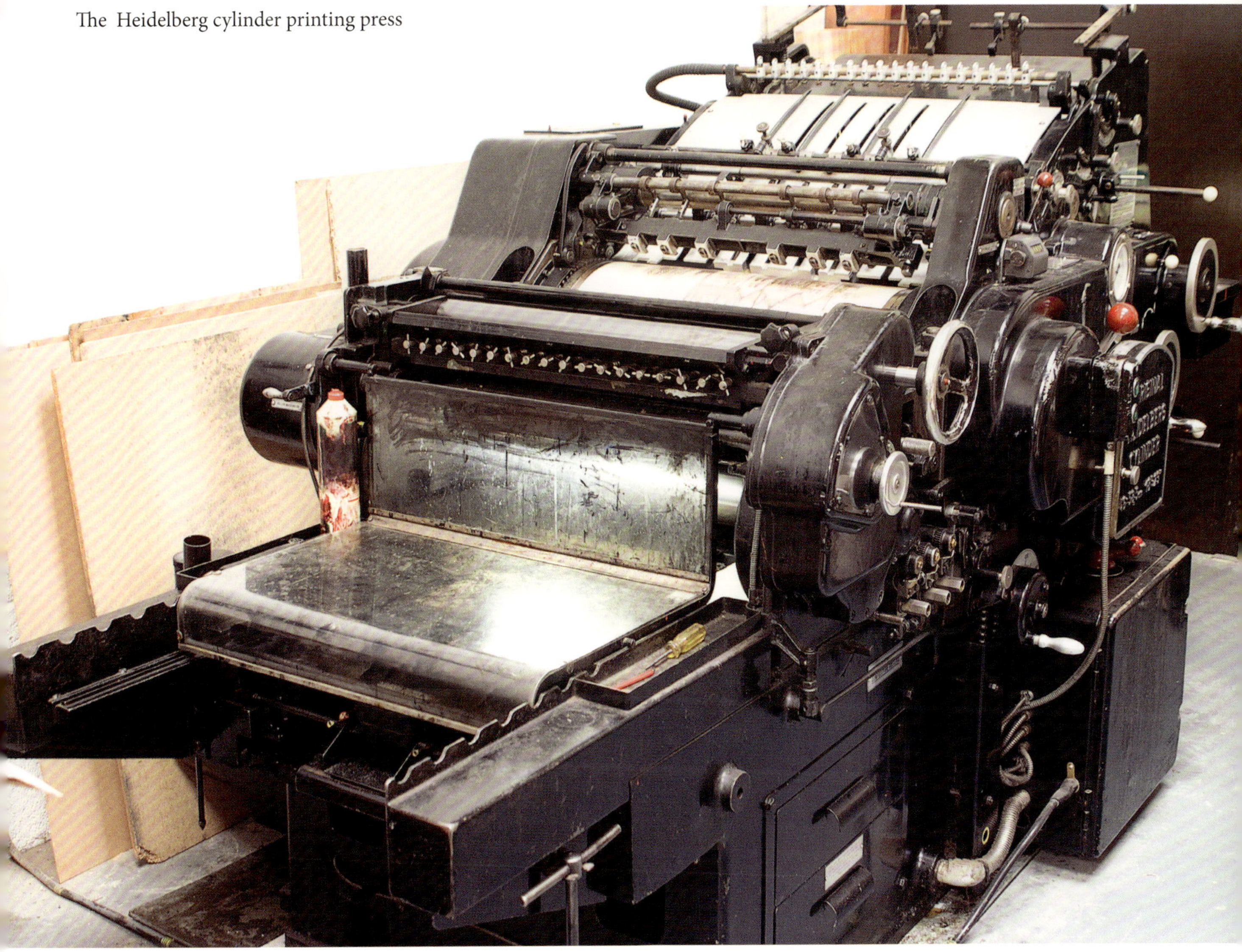

Piles of part finished prints awaiting the final colour

Patrick Roe at The Logan Press with the Heidelberg press used for printing the colour plates

Printer Brian Watkin examining proofs and the progression of colour with Fiona Kelly (née Toplis) the artist's great-granddaughter, also her daughter Aoife

David and Fiona Kelly with the printers at The Logan Press comparing final proofs and 1908 prints

Aluminium backed plate mounted on the honeycomb ready for printing while quality is checked for the previous plate

Betty Roberts at The Fine Book Bindery mounting finished prints on the backing paper and 'tipping in' the printed tissue overlays

Typesetting and Text Printing

There are very few professional typesetters or printers who can still produce letterpress printing in the style and quality of the original *Book of Sark*. Stan Lane at Gloucester Typesetting and John Grice at Evergreen Press are a very rare combination with more than 90 years experience between them and probably the last of their kind! Neither has apprentices and if we had not had their help now it is doubtful if *The Centenary Book of Sark* could have been produced in as authentic a manner.

Notes on a visit to their offices in Stroud by Chris Andrews, Thursday 2nd July 2009:

'Absolutely knocked out by the work of John and Stan. Have just come back from a visit there, baking hot day, drove over to review a first proof of a typeset page.

Firstly, the set up is very atmospheric, in an old mill by a river and the Stroudwater canal. The mill itself has important print history – it was the only one in the world to manufacture 'flong' a paper mache like substance used in early rotary printing.

Our meeting held to a background of nesting swallows twittering as they flew around, and sometimes through the open windows. John's printing area is a spacious, light room with large windows and well ventilated. John explained much about the appearance of the new page when compared with the old. We were reviewing the text for the picture "The West Coast" which they have reset and printed. When one looks closely at one of the original books the typesetting is of a certain style, with distinctive spacing inserted to accommodate the text justified left and right and giving a light and airy feel with the generous margins on the page. We all feel it important to reflect the craft of the original setting and our mantra is always 'if in doubt be consistent but above all, stick with the original'. There are still some anomalies, look closely at page 23 (or 94 and others in a 1908 volume) the inverted commas are exactly that, "quote marks" probably did not exist as a concept when the book was set, so the commas were simply put upside down. In the original book the leading set is also larger than the trailing – we follow this style. In rare instances the type is imperfect, page 47 has a broken f, there is a strangely bold M on page x and a missing dot over the i on page xi in the word 'possession'. In some cases a more decorative form of the same letter has been used, in particular the use of a 'swash', the curved addition for instance to a letter, as here with the A and R of Royal Academy.

A MONARCH OF THE SHORE, SARK. (GRANDE GRÈVE)

From the Oil Painting in the possession of James Dixon, Esq., exhibited in the Royal Academy, 1902.

GOULIOT ROCKS, COAST OF SARK

From the Oil Painting in the possession of S. Copestake, Esq., exhibited in the Royal Academy, 1884.

Details from the preliminary pages of the 1908 edition showing the 'swashes' on the A's and R's above, but the standard version below

We looked at all the type and sizes, the majority of the text is in 18pt Caslon, half-title pages are in 24pt, but the text page headings themselves are in 22pt. This is a rarer size and 24pt had been used for our test. It was agreed if the 22pt could be found that would be better, and it is what now appears in

The Centenary Edition of The Book of Sark. *It was further noted that the initial letter of each text page was a different fount, slightly elongated and finer than the Caslon capitals. Again it was agreed if this could be matched then this should be done, and it has been. Letter spacing was seen in the titling as being a little eccentric as was the punctuation in the text. We no longer use spaces before colons, semi-colons or exclamation marks as they did 100 years ago but again the mantra of 'stick with the original' was agreed and this was slavishly done in all cases. Finally it was noted in the 1908 text that* Toplis's *was used for the possessive rather than* Toplis' *which is used in the commentary volume.*

Text pages from an unbound original copy of The Book of Sark *were supplied by the Kelly family as the typesetting guide. The typesetting and casting work by Stan is quite extraordinary. He works on a pneumatic keyboard which looks a little like a tilted typewriter, on which he produces a punched tape to operate the Monotype caster. The caster itself is a beautiful piece of engineering which produces individual letters in single lines from molten metal – a mix of lead, antimony and tin. These are then checked and made up by hand with margins and spacing to match the original pages. I thought John's area was full, until I saw Stan's typesetting machine and then his casting area. He must surely be a very rare craftsman indeed now. He loves his job and enthusiasm shone out of him even though, as he said, he had been in the job for 54 years.*

We were able to agree the overall style of The Centenary Edition, *it is above all an amazingly fine and accurate reproduction of the original* Book of Sark *and no expense has been spared in ensuring it is of absolute archival quality.'*

Stan Lane explains the intricacy of the caster to Mike Brain (designer of this book) and above, an ingot of metal being fed into the 'hot metal' pot

Stan Lane keying the text

Monitoring the caster

Examining the cast type

Finished type

John Grice at the press with an older hand operated press in the foreground

Mounting a text page on the printing impression cylinder of the press, the type bed in the foreground

Taking out the printed sheet

The Text Paper

A test making of paper gave material to make up a dummy and print the first couple of text pages. In discussion it was agreed the feel of the paper and overall look of the pages was lovely, but even though an original had been carefully measured at the St Cuthbert's Paper Mill and the bulk of the new paper was a match, it did not quite appear the same. Ironically this is because the new paper is so much better than the original. The older paper has more impurities in it and probably also contained wood pulp as opposed to cotton. The new paper is slightly softer and a little less opaque. So a new dummy of a few sections was produced using a much heavier paper, 250gsm rather than the measured 190gsm. The physical feel and opacity of the paper is now excellent, and its added bulk means *The Book of Sark Centenary Edition* is slightly weightier than the original, with enhanced feel and appearance.

Chris Andrews examining the initial paper samples at The Logan Press

The process of making the paper for *The Book of Sark Centenary Edition* is briefly illustrated on the following pages.

St Cuthbert's Mill

Cotton, the main constituent of the paper

Cotton pulp, known as 'stuff'

The newly formed paper as it leaves the cylinder mould and is transferred to a roller

Paper feeding into the 'calendar stacks' for producing the correct texture

The paper making machine manufactured in 1908

Finished paper is fed to a roll at the end of the machine

Texture comparison and check of the shade of finished paper under special lighting

Trimming to sheets

Final hand check of individual sheets and packing

Hand Book Binding by Derry's of Nottingham.

The following is an outline description with illustrations of the final stages of the book production.

Andy Graves rounding the spine of the book block with a traditional binder's hammer. The book block is the collated, glued collection of the text and plate mounting pages

Attaching decorative head and tail bands using acid free neutral adhesive. Acid free paper is attached to overlap the head and tail bands and one side of the book block

The natural classic vellum is cut to overlap the pre-cut bookboards then glued to the boards

Positioning the pre-cut book boards on the book block to check fit and confirm size

The vellum and book boards are put in a press to ensure adhesion and removal of air bubbles

Michael Webster removing the excess gold leaf after blocking the design onto the front cover in a press

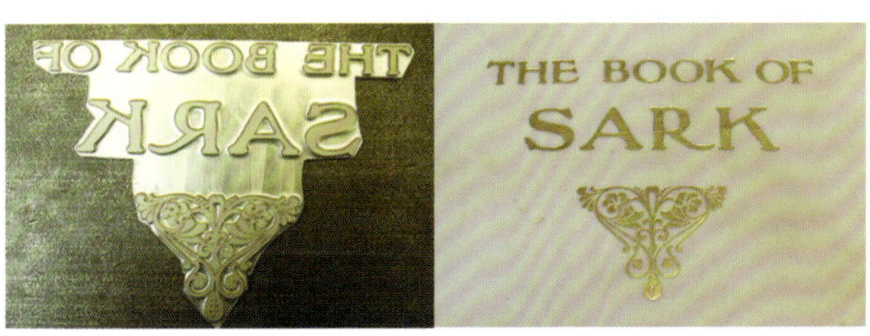

The metal die and finished result of the front cover

Ribbons are threaded through the foredge of the case

The case is glued to the book block

The finished book is pressed between French joint boards

The books are left overnight, removed from the press, tied with cord to ensure no movement of the glueing and are then inserted into the Solander Box.

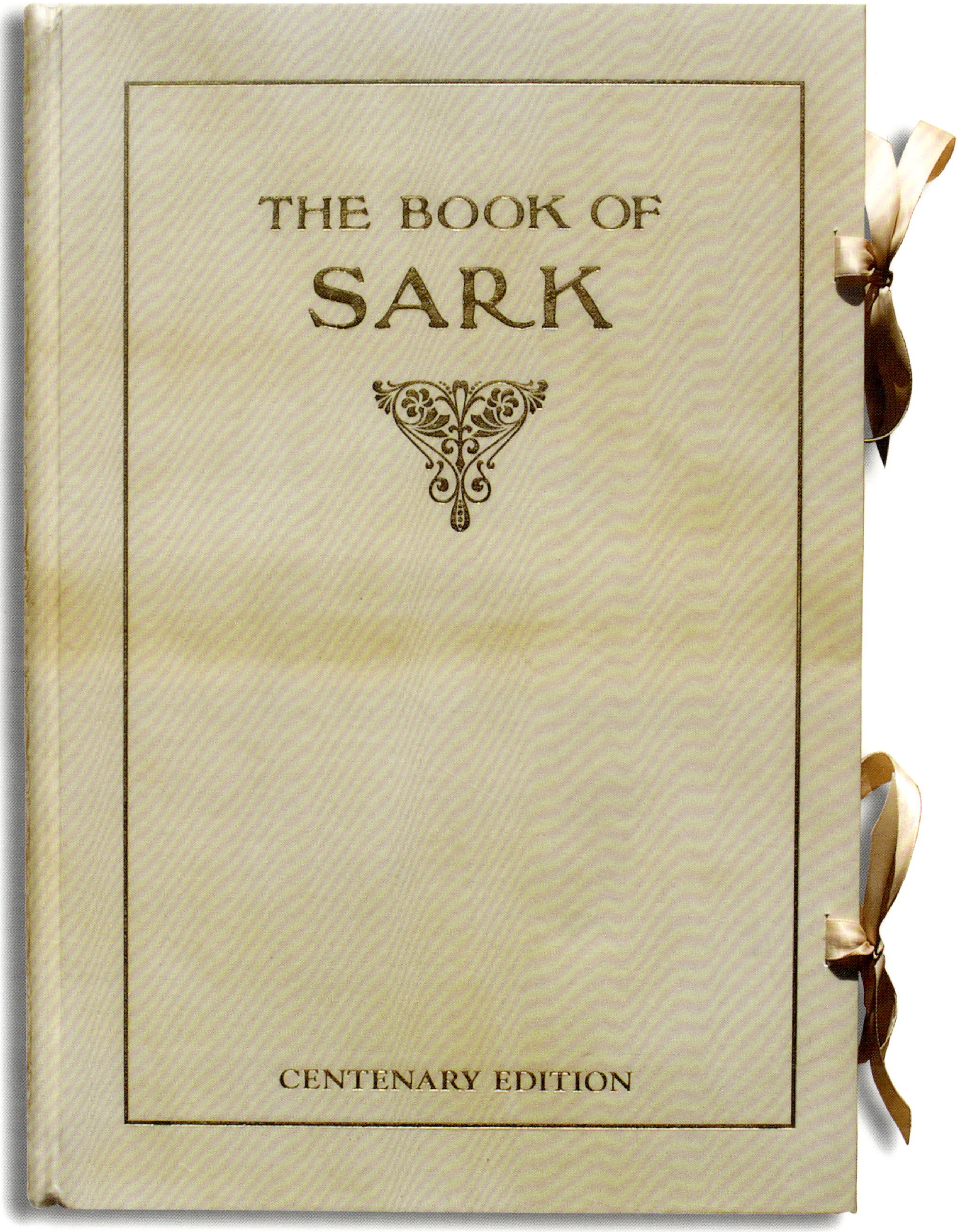
THE BOOK OF
SARK
CENTENARY EDITION

Section 4
Toplis' Prints and a Contemporary Photographic Comparison of the Views

Toplis' Views 100 Years after Publication, Notes on Access, Changes, and the Challenges Involved in Making a Comparison

Toplis often took many years over his paintings and it became more and more evident that the earlier description of him visiting and revisiting sites was accurate, so a caveat to viewing all of the comparison photographs is that they represent the best that can be done as a copy of the scenes he painted. Hopefully the geographical features are shown well and at the correct tide but the different appearance of weather, light and time of day may leave something to stimulate the reader's imagination in order to form their comparison.

Toplis often painted as though viewing scenes through a very wide angle lens, sometimes somewhat selectively applied – see The West Coast of Sark painting and the size of Brecqhou – though there is absolutely no evidence he used a camera at any time. Indeed a preliminary sketch of a version of this view, (see page 12) shows something of his meticulous method of working.

None of the photographs are altered in order to more closely 'mimic' Toplis' work. The views are as seen, and the readers have the opportunity to exercise their imagination as to artistic licence.

These descriptions were written on a sunny day in Oxford, sitting at an office studio desk with Toplis' pictures and photographic images displayed together on the computer. Behind on a bench was a copy of the 1908 *Book of Sark,* opened at the relevant page to enable exact reference to colour and composition which the computer screen might otherwise change. A print of the photograph and the 1908 Toplis print were reviewed. It was only when seen side by side that the true comparison – and if necessary notes for a better comparison could be made.

In the following pages mention of Oxenham's text is made and selective quotes which may aid comparison are reproduced in italics. More information may be gained by reading all of his text as reproduced in *The Book of Sark Centenary Edition.*

Above and here, finding the 'Toplis location' at Port Gorey (or Gouray as spelt by Oxenham)

Location photography at the arch on Grande Grève for the picture A Monarch of the Shore, and a view through the arch. Photographs on these two pages by Reese Andrews

Creux Harbour, Sark

In making a comparison of the first photograph to the Toplis print, look at the relationship of the "V" of the rocks behind the quay, Toplis' view shows the quay head on the left ending at the base of the "V", but the relation of the rocks behind to the harbour wall and steps is not correct in the photograph. The round harbour wall we now see was an extension when the new wall on the right hand side was built. Oxenham's commentary notes this: *'The outjutting arm of weed-fringed rock is now covered with masonry like the quay-head opposite, and the quay itself rebuilt.'*

After much examination of the Toplis picture and the view, it was concluded that the relationship of the "V" and the end of the harbour quay wall was misleading – because of the extension and rebuilding. Also it needs a wider view (as Toplis' vision) and the position needs to be several yards to the left and slightly lower – but – was the level of the quay raised as well – or is it just the difference between a short artist sitting at an easel and a photographer standing upright?

To improve the comparison the view was re-photographed at a lower tide in summer in afternoon light and though there may be compromises, it seems accurate in its composition. Though in the text relating to the painting, Oxenham remarked, *'The picture was painted, under many difficulties of time and circumstance, for the sole purpose of preserving to old lovers of Sark a disappearing landmark.'*

The comparison on the following pages shows how the harbour has changed since the painting was completed, most obviously with the second wall on the right hand side, but also the left hand quay being extended and enlarged. The zig zag path on the headland behind is still clear and unchanged.

N.B. Here and throughout this commentary volume a copy of the Toplis print from one of the new *Centenary Edition* books is reproduced, the viewer will be able to see a change when compared with prints in the 1908 *Book of Sark*.

A further quote from Oxenham:

'But it is the water that is in the Creux that is a perpetual delight. It is, indeed the same living liquid crystal which we find everywhere else about the island, so sparkling, vitally clear,'

First attempt at the comparison photograph

Creux Harbour, Sark

Toplis print

The 2008 photographic comparison

The Creux Tunnel, Sark

The Toplis print

Initially it was hard to believe the Toplis view was not the old tunnel, it does look like his painting – see opposite. However, reading the *Book of Sark* text indicates clearly it is the new tunnel that Toplis has recorded *'and the new one, here depicted by Mr. Toplis, was pierced on a level with the landing stage in 1868.'*

The view changed markedly soon after Toplis painted it and this was not universally popular Oxenham's text sayes: *'The recently-added granite facing to the archway may possibly serve some occult purpose, but from the artistic point of view it is nothing but an eyesore.'*

Now the archway has again been renovated, and the tunnel has interior walls. Richard Axton, archivist at La Société Sercquaise writes: *'So far as I can gather the new tunnel was faced in granite between 1898, when Toplis painted it, and 1908 when Oxenham laments the aesthetic. The facing appears in Edwardian photos of the steamer in Creux. Records of Chief Pleas from 8th April 1931 show that £1,248 was voted for lining the tunnel. Some people say that the German occupiers did the concrete lining, but this seems only have been repairs.'*

The photograph shown overleaf seems to closely mimic the artist's viewpoint, but the intervening changes have made it almost unrecognisable. The white painting to the opening, the addition of various sheds and bikes outside the tunnel entrance and the concreting inside give a much different appearance. Also there is a café on the spot where Oxenham mentions a *'limekiln'*, but the *'Creux Road'* can still be clearly seen running upwards behind.

Views of the old tunnel showing that though they look similar these pictures are not the same construction, or view that Toplis painted

The Creux Tunnel, Sark

Toplis print

The 2008 photographic comparison

Old Well at Dixcart, Sark

Getting to the area of this picture proved less of a challenge than some, but the actual view proved more tricky and straddling the muddy little stream that now issues from the well was eventually found to be the right position. However it provided an object lesson in why not to wear pale clothing while photographing in Sark, especially in slippery conditions.

The path towards Dixcart Valley and the wells. Stocks Hotel in the distance

There are actually a number of wells in the Dixcart Valley in the area that the description indicates and all are quite close together. Oxenham says: *'The Old Well lies in a green nook almost buried in fern and bramble.'* It is certainly very overgrown and surrounded by more trees now and soon it will be overwhelmed and possibly form part of an ambitious expansion building for the nearby hotel.

'The Old Well' from the new building site

There are several wells close together in the Dixcart Valley, but this is not the one Toplis painted

Old Well at Dixcart, Sark

Toplis print

The 2008 photographic comparison

Dixcart Bay, Sark

Dixcart Bay offers a relatively accessible view with a clear path to the beach, though it is demanding in places. Perhaps the main difference over the years is that the beach profile has evolved and the mix of stone sizes changed. Dixcart is a stone beach and is affected by the tides and weather conditions. The Toplis perspective is even wider than the photograph, hence the greater diminution of size of the coast behind the arch and the size of The Barracks, where the Toplis family lived for a while, which is just visible on the left hand edge.

It is not surprising though that the beach profile has changed. Look at the winter view at low tide of this area. The sea has removed almost all the stones and scraped the beach down to a few larger rocks and sand underneath. This all changed again in the summer when the comparison photograph was taken and the picture painted.

Some rock has fallen from inside the arch, enlarging it a little. Also changed is the left hand outer edge of the arch and a smoothing of the top jagged edge, not, perhaps what Oxenham expected: '*the fine natural arch ... rugged in its architecture as though reared by giant hands to last throughout all time*'.

Winter view of The Dixcart Bay and Arch

Dixcart Bay, Sark

Toplis print

The 2008 photographic comparison

The West Coast of Sark

'This view of the west coast, from a little coign of vantage on the Eperquerie Headland, not far from the Chimney entrance to the Boutiques, is, I think, quite unrivalled'. Oxenham's opening paragraph is apt and as well as commending the view, notes one of the several instances where it seemed possible to find a small feature, maybe a rock platform or seat where Toplis might well have sat and painted. Indeed here there was a very strong feel of his presence as the '*coign of vantage*' was found and the scene unfolded.

The '*coign of vantage*' where Toplis painted

The view along the west coast to '*the coign*'

One contemporary copy of the Toplis view, the main change being the large building now on Brecqhou. Most features on the cliffs seem unchanged, the path and old wall on the two headlands are particularly notable and still clear, as they were 100 years ago. This and the comparison overleaf are photographed at a slightly lower tide than when Toplis painted, which means a rock shows in the middle of the bay.

Detail view of the wall and track on the second headland in the above picture, as clear as it was in Toplis' day

The West Coast of Sark

Toplis print

The 2008 photographic comparison

Nature's Architecture, Sark (Port du Moulin)

Toplis print

The 2008 photographic comparison. Extraordinarily elegant and strong, perhaps the arch has lost some stone, but it stays distinctive and clear

Les Autelets, Ile De Serk (And Saignée Cliffs)

Toplis print

A demanding scramble to reach the view, Oxenham writes: *'Crawling humbly on hands and knees over chaotic boulders the size of cottages, slipping hazardously on the polished weed-slides between the Autelets and the stupendous cliffs'.*
When the photographer was making his way to this view he found the description particularly apt. The rocks are large, weedy and very slippery. The progress was slow and constant falling meant man and equipment were as often on the floor as upright

The 2008 photographic comparison

A careful review of the Toplis print and the scene. This was a challenging photograph but shows clearly how much has changed, yet how much has stayed the same

La Saignée, Sark

Toplis print

'La Saignée, however, is rich in colouring besides its barbaric black and gold,' Oxenham is right, but the original painting's colours are probably not as exaggerated as the print. The set of proofs of this view from the original 1908 printing, to the right, show a progression of increasing saturation of the red and yellow. Perhaps this went too far and indicates again the reason for the continual rejection of proofs by Toplis.

Three printed proofs of this view from the 1908 printing showing how the colour was increased to try and achieve the result Toplis wanted

The 2008 photographic comparison

Oxenham again comments on the colour in detail, '*And the interior colouring! Jasper-green and deep blood-red–fresh deep red, as though some awful deed had been wrought within the rock or on the cliffs above*'. Close up photographs within the archway at the southern corner of the bay show something perhaps that Toplis was trying to indicate in his tone and colour.

Les Autelets, Sark

Toplis print

The 2008 photographic comparison

A Sark Souffleur (Saignée Bay)

Toplis print

The Souffleur only works around the high tide during a strong north-west gale and Saignée Bay is impossible to get to in these conditions. Arguably it is worse now than in Toplis' time, due to the fall of the cliff path. Even then, Oxenham writes:

'(the Souffleur) can also be seen with little difficulty–unless, indeed, a full gale be blowing–from the cliff-path, on the south side of Saignée Bay. The picture of course represents the souffleur as seen from the beach below, but he would be a bold climber who would venture the treacherous zigzag path in its present condition. In storm-time it is absolutely dangerous.'

This then, would appear to be the only work where Toplis has not painted the scene exactly as he saw it, but used imagination and memory. He did however, make his own path to Saignée, hence the large number of paintings from this bay.

The photograph opposite gives a view of the Souffleur fully working, (courtesy of William Raymond) as well as views of the Souffleur cave in the cliffs.

The souffleur working

The souffleur cave from the shore

The headland with the cave in the foreground

La Cave De La Fontaine, Sark (Fern Cave)

Oxenham's description of how to get to this view:

'Down a long green slope north of the Creux Belet, over the cliff by a path hidden in bramble and bracken, down a zigzag till we strike the rocks, and so at last to the boulder strewn shore. And still the Fern Cave may be long sought for and yet not found.'

It is certainly true that the cave is hard to find and it was fortunate to have the knowledgeable help of Susan Synott in finding this and in showing the way to the Fairy Grotto that is the next Toplis view and comparison in this book. Oxenham continues his description, mentioning the access round a

The '*huge fallen rock*' at the entrance to the cave

'huge fallen rock', and goes on to describe the atmosphere and colours to be seen within the cave thus: *'dark-green, brown, white, orange, blood-red, amber, and black ;'*

These colours may indeed be seen, by looking in detail at the rock, small areas are quite bright and full of contrast, but in the photograph they do not seem to attain the appearance of the print.

Colour details in the walls of the cave

Perhaps one of the most interesting comparisons of any of the Toplis pictures and the comparison photograph is on the next page, in that the Marine Spleenwort is still to be seen and very much in a similar position and extent as it was 100 years ago: *'whose delicate fronds cluster thick in the vault of the roof and depend like soft green fringe from every ledge'*. This is an older usage of the word depend, meaning to descend – from.

La Cave De La Fontaine, Sark (Fern Cave)

Toplis print

The painting appears as if from a slightly higher perspective than it is possible to photograph from, because of the overhang of the large rock at the entrance. Perhaps Toplis preferred the lines in the rock on the left leading straight into the composition and was able to alter his perspective or possibly the rock has moved in the 100 years that separate these images

The 2008 photographic comparison

A Fairy Grotto, Sark

The way over the rock strewn beach. The arch contains the 'Fairy' shape when seen through the cave from the other side

For this view, as the one of the The Fern Cave, thanks are due to Susan Synnot, who kindly led the expedition and showed the views. Oxenham suggests access by way of the rocky shore around from the Fern Cave, it may also be reached and perhaps slightly easier, by way over the rocks below and to the right of the Eperquerie Landing.

The comparison shows the 'Fairy' arch has lost a little stone inside but many rock shapes are recognisable. The colour issue of the printing is very marked with this view and the comparison may be seen between the Toplis original painting, the reproduction in the 1908 *Book of Sark* and the current reproduction from the plates. If the detail photographs are compared with Toplis' original painting something of his colour is evident, perhaps again, he looked closely at the rocks and decided to bring out the colour a little more that he saw in detail?

The expedition to the Fairy Grotto led to one of the more moving discoveries. Chris Andrews tells the story:

'There was a marvellous moment as we came to this view, scrambling round the rocks the composition was emerging and as I manoeuvred to try and get exactly Toplis' perspective I realised there was a natural seat with a small ledge in front and to the left. This might give weight to the thought that we were exactly in the right spot. Then finally I saw at the bottom of that area the rusted remains of an iron peg, driven into the a rock cleft below the ledge. Could this be an anchor for the artist's easel? I felt a distinct frisson, a shiver of excitement as I sat, surely exactly where Toplis did, 100 years ago.'

The view emerging as the rocks were climbed, the natural ledge and the metal pin

A Fairy Grotto, Sark

Toplis print

The 2008 photographic comparison

Guliot Rocks, Coast of Sark

It is a true scramble to get to this. The faint path to the Guliot caves goes round a steep friable shoulder of rock. There is a large stone in the path that exactly marks this view. It seems substantially as the artist's depiction and perhaps he used it as his viewpoint. He certainly painted from the path as Oxenham writes: *'Mr. Toplis's picture is painted from this footpath, just where it rounds the slope'.*

Toplis print

Path and rock, just where it rounds the slope

The 2008 photographic comparison

Grève De La Ville, Sark

If viewed critically the comparison picture in this case is not totally accurate, not only for its content, but in the manner of its production. Notes from the day:

'The photograph ended up being taken half way up a tree and leaning out towards the cliff edge. The fact that it was taken at all owes a good deal to the local knowledge and persistence of the guide that day, Jess Hester. Oxenham's only clue to the location is the phrase "from the downs above Grève de la Ville". *Well, this is no longer very practical as these downs are thickly wooded with the addition of impenetrable weavings of bracken and bramble. The closest approximation to the viewpoint was in the tree. There was no way to continue further up and round the area to improve the perspective to the same as Toplis. But it proved an entertaining exercise in getting as far as possible and the scratches and other minor injuries will doubtless fade in time.'*

Jess Hester and the tree used to obtain the best view

Impenetrable slopes from the downs above the bay

An initial view from the main path to the bay, but the composition is different from the Toplis painting

Grève De La Ville, Sark

Toplis print

The 2008 photographic comparison

La Coupée, Sark

Toplis print

The 2008 photographic comparison

It is likely there have been significant rock falls since Toplis painted this. The cliffs are far from stable as a recent (early 2010) fall on the other side that closed the path down to Grande Grève Bay and altered the whole appearance of the rock face proved. Toplis may have had a larger and higher point to paint from, alternatively it may be an illusion because the roadway has been built up and the railings added, altering the perception of the view. It may also have been that this is an example where Toplis made use of a platform, lowered on ropes from the cliff above, to paint from. He is known to have had one made and apparently persuaded, or ordered, his sons to transport it about for him.

His composition is so wide that more than one exposure has been combined to make this comparison image.

A Wintry Morning on the Coupée, Sark

Toplis print

Oxenham's text describes the atmosphere and the view:

'In the long sweeping slopes and tumbling scarps of the Coupée, with their strenuous heights and depths and the lonely bays and hollows beyond, there is, even on a soft summer day, something solemn and majestic, something at once awe-inspiring and uplifting.

The sight of them draped in snow—a sight not seen more than once or twice in a lifetime—must be as wonderful as it is rare, and never to be forgotten by the privileged few.

Then, with a leaden sea heaving sombrely under a leaden grey sky, the lonely depths show grim and bleak indeed. The silence is like the silence of death ;'

The 2008 photographic comparison

This winter comparison is not exactly the Toplis viewpoint but it shows the Coupée well in a truly seasonal light. Photo courtesy of Richard Axton.

On the Hills in Sark, Autumn

Toplis print

'Here on the hillside below the Cromlech—so-called, but of somewhat doubtful authenticity—we sit looking along the south-west coast and downs towards Guernsey.'

This may be a rare occurrence of Oxenham being mistaken in his text, as this is the south-east coast of Little Sark, though possibly looking in the general direction of Guernsey. However the doubted Cromlech is still in evidence and the walk past La Sablonnerie and on, in the direction of Rouge Terrier is pleasant and calm as he later states:

'But autumn in Little Sark has a charm entirely its own—the charm of wide-reaching solitudes unbroken by any sign of man or his handiwork.'

The way to the Cromlech, right, past signposts for Rouge Terrier and silver mine ruins

The 2008 photographic comparison

A cliff fall prevents access to a lower perpective for this photograph but the features shown indicate how well Toplis observed detail, including the diagonal wall, which, though a little more overgrown in the 100 years is still clearly visible.

The view north from the Cromlech is spectacular too, perhaps it was glancing at this that inspired Toplis for the 'Baleine Bay' picture, which is substantially this, but from a window in The Barracks, his then home and studio.
Toplis used the Cromlech as a store and would sometimes leave all his painting equipment here at the end of a day, then return the next day to continue painting

Venus's Bath (or as styled in full in the 1908 *Book*: "Formed and adorned by Nature's wondrous Art, A Sea-shore pool—to 'Venus' dedicate")

Toplis print

This is one of the most accurate of the Toplis paintings in almost every aspect. The new printing of the plates brought a great result, the rock shapes and lines are minutely detailed and accurate. The fringe of lighter coloured seaweed in the bottom right, where the artist signed his work is visible and still to be seen in the photograph today. Perhaps the only evidence of artistic licence is the rock and pebble rendering on the floor of the pool, which has been said to be there because the artist dropped

The 2008 photographic comparison

his brush on to the painting when he had felt the work was finished and the resulting smudge had to be corrected, so he painted pebbles which had been brought back to his studio and substituted them for the otherwise clear and accurate rendition of reflections from the rocks above. (see also page 20 and 21).

Baleine Bay, Sark

Toplis print

The 2008 photographic comparison

The comparison photograph here is believed to be from exactly the place Toplis sat to paint. The description in the 1908 *Book of Sark* from Oxenham indicates when referring to the viewpoint for this picture: *'The back window of the row of cottages ... commands a wonderful view of Sark,'* this *'row of cottages'* is the building known as The Barracks on Little Sark where the Artist lived for a while and the back window is still identifiable. The gable end of the *'dilapidated shed,'* is prominent (perhaps too prominent) in the foreground, the composition seems very accurate, with perhaps a little artistic change to the perspective to bring the far bays a little closer? But the main changes evident are the buildings seen above and to the left of Dixcart Bay and the further dilapidation of the shed.

Port Gouray, Sark

Toplis print

The photographic view is less tranquil than the painted scene but the very great accuracy of the composition is evident when the relationship between the rocky pinnacle in the foreground is compared to the inlet and promentaries behind, also the relationship of the cliff edge to the right with

The 2008 photographic comparison

the offshore islets. Perhaps the most noticeable change is a large increase in the coverage of the cliff by gorse which made the descent to this viewpoint a delicate matter, but well rewarded with one of Little Sark's most attractive sea views. (see also page 66).

A Monarch of the Shore, Grande Grève, Sark

Toplis print

Toplis may be a few feet higher than the photographic comparison, as indicated by the area of sea visible through the arch and beyond the sea shore. The rock distribution and profile of the shore must have changed somewhat since his time, but the small rock balanced above the centre cleft of the arch still remains.

The 2008 photographic comparison

As ever there is great detail in the Toplis' recording of rock shapes and markings and his frustration at the original colour rendition of his work, which again seems very red and ochre, can only be imagined. It is noted with apology, that despite great perseverance, no seagull could be persuaded to fly through the arch at an appropriate moment for the photographer.

The Editions and Originals Compared

The following pages show a selected comparison of prints from the 1908 *Book of Sark* and the *The Book of Sark Centenary Edition,* shown alongside a reproduction of the few actual originals available now that were used to make the plates. Note: the appearance of the original paintings will have been affected by ageing of the covering varnish.

A Fairy Grotto, Sark

Toplis original

1908 Edition print

Centenary Edition print

Guliot Rocks, Coast of Sark

Toplis original

1908 Edition print

Centenary Edition print

La Cave De La Fontaine, Sark (Fern Cave)

Toplis original

1908 Edition print

Centenary Edition print

Dixcart Bay, Sark

Toplis original

1908 Edition print

Centenary Edition print

The Centenary Edition Images

Creux Harbour, Sark

The Creux Tunnel, Sark

Dixcart Bay, Sark

Nature's Architecture, Sark
(Port du Moulin)

Les Autelets, Sark

La Cave De La Fontaine, Sark
(Fern Cave)

A Fairy Grotto, Sark

Guliot Rocks, Coast of Sark

Grève De La Ville, Sark

Venus's Bath

Port Gouray, Sark

A Monarch of the Shore, Grande Grève, Sark

Old Well at Dixcart, Sark

The West Coast of Sark

Les Autelets, Ile De Serk (And Saignée Cliffs)

La Saignée, Sark

A Sark Souffleur (Saignée Bay)

La Coupée, Sark

A Wintry Morning on the Coupée, Sark

On the Hills in Sark, Autumn

Baleine Bay, Sark

Publishing The Book of Sark, Centenary Edition *has been an extraordinary experience. The time taken has spanned the centenary of publication, from nearly two years before to nearly two years after. It has involved in some cases the last generation of British craftsmen capable of producing the work required, in the style and quality to match the original and in most respects to achieve improvements.*

The reproduction of Toplis' work is as good as can be achieved, the text is a faithful following of the content and style, the printing and binding have all been carried out on genuine archival British material by dedicated British craftsmen. This is a unique production which is beautiful now and will be enjoyed for generations to come.

- CHRIS ANDREWS
Publisher

GATEWAY PUBLISHING LTD
19 85
SARK